"Dixieland Gangs & Disruptive Groups:
Crime & Impact on the Southeast United States"

By Gabe Morales

© 2016

Table of Contents

"It is curious that physical courage should be so common in the world, and moral courage so rare." – Mark Twain

Introduction

As a geographic location within the United States, "Dixie" is usually defined as the eleven Southern states that seceded from the Union in late 1860 and early 1861 to form the Confederate States of America. These states were: South Carolina, Mississippi, Florida, Alabama, Georgia, Louisiana, Texas, Virginia, Arkansas, North Carolina, and Tennessee. Dixieland is often referred to as hot jazz or traditional jazz, is a style based on the music that developed in New Orleans at the start of the 20th century. In this case, we refer to the land of Dixie or "Dixieland", focusing on gang activity in the "Deep South".

This book includes the history of disruptive groups and street gangs active within this area from mid-1800s to date, but one cannot understand well their origins or why they exist today without understanding the history of the South. It is for this reason the first three chapters include a lot of history of politics in the Deep South.

Street gang formation was often an urban phenomenon with the first street gangs being documented in New York City in the early 1800s. The advent of street gangs in the Deep South lagged far behind those in the North, or even in places in the Southwest like El Paso, Texas. Exceptions would be organized crime in places like "The Big Easy" New Orleans (1900) and "Cigar City" Tampa, FL (1946).

In fact, in a 1970, a U.S. Department of Justice study was conducted of "Fifteen large metropolitan areas with youth gang survey cities" to evaluate gang problems in what was considered a representative sampling of U.S. cities. As a result, none in that group were located south of Washington, D.C.-MD-VA, nor were any in the southern part of the country east of Houston, TX. That is not to say there were not dangerous criminals predating the FBI's Most Wanted List (1949) or that disruptive groups like the KKK (1865) were not present in the South prior to 1970.

Crime groups in the southeast portion of the United States run from fairly unorganized groups like "Moonshine Operations", to full-fledged street gangs, prison gangs, motorcycle gangs, and organized crime. While they may not meet the definition of a "street gang", criminal groups in the southern part of the United States have existed much longer than most people realize.

The James-Younger Gang was a notable 19th-century gang of American outlaws that included notorious outlaw Jesse James. The gang had its origins in a group of

Confederate bushwhackers who fought in the bitter partisan fighting that wracked the state of Missouri during the American Civil War and was centered in the state of Missouri and home of most of its members. The gang's main crime was robbery. They would usually commit these robberies during horse mounted raids usually separated by many months of inactivity and laying low in nearby areas.

My mother's side of the family were Arkies. Arkansas is well known for hidden treasures. During the 1800's, the KGC (Knights of the Golden Circle), as well as outlaw Jessie James, were known to have buried many treasures within Arkansas.

In the late 1800s, Myra "Belle Starr" Reed was known as a notorious female outlaw in America's "Old West." As a resident of Indian Territory, she came under the jurisdiction of Judge Isaac C. Parker in Fort Smith, Arkansas. Starr's closer associates included the legendary American outlaws Cole Younger and Frank and Jesse James. Her reputation as an outlaw, the novelty of being a woman outlaw, and her violent, mysterious death led to her being called "The Bandit Queen."

Most members of street gangs today (in contrast to Outlaw Motorcycle Gangs, Domestic Extremist, etc.) are minorities, specifically African-American and Hispanic. This is no different today in the South than in most of the United States.

Prior to the 1970s, most street gangs in America consisted of the sons, and sometimes daughters, of Jewish, Irish, Italian, Polish, German, and other European-Americans. Walter B. Miller, an expert on gang matters, found that by 1975, the membership of most U.S. gangs were no longer White. Miller's work was documented in a pilot National Youth Gang Survey, which found high levels of gang violence in New York, Chicago, Los Angeles, Detroit, Philadelphia, and San Francisco, among other cities, and showed a shift in demographics of the typical gang member.

Of the four national origins Miller identified (African, Asian, European, not Hispanic, and Hispanic, approximately half of the gang members in the cities deemed to have gang problems were African-American, about one-sixth were Hispanic, only one-tenth were Asian, and another one-tenth were European, not Hispanic (White). So, altogether, about 80% of the gang members in the 1970s were African-American or Hispanic.

The history of African-American gang members in the U.S., including the Southeast, is often traced to the post-Civil Rights movement. We propose that we should go further back, to pre-Civil War days to lay out why many Blacks today feel there are two Americas, one Black, and one White. A large influx of African-Americans came to the U.S. as slaves prior to the U.S. Civil War (1861-1865), so we will address the dispersion of that group in the first chapter as a lead into what happened later.

A growing number of U.S. gang members today are Chicano/Latino, and the South, to the surprise of many people, is also seeing a large growth of Hispanic gangs.

Street gangs are often formed as the result of marginalization, limiting access to social and economic conditions. Marginalization refers to the process of pushing someone to the edge of a group, relegating him or her to a powerless position of lesser importance. This is often a social phenomenon, in which a minority group is excluded. Respected sociologists Gregory Brown, James Vigil, and Eric Taylor learned that marginalization especially affected children, "in the aftermath of the migration of ethnically distinct populations."

I researched material in-depth, and interviewed numerous individuals, including gang members and local law enforcement, in particular nationwide gang expert Hunter "Gator" Glass, Adam Schniper who was a past President of the Alabama Gang Investigators Association, and Carter F. Smith who was a Founding Board Member of the Tennessee Gang Investigators Association, to give you an up to date picture of gangs in the southeast United States and their impact on crime and communities.

I hope you find this book to be useful…Stay safe!

Sincerely,

Gabriel C. Morales (at an old Tennessee Plantation House)

Foreword

Now here we go, finally an exceptionally researched and easy to read book on the topic of gangs. Gabe Morales has truly outdone himself this time. No longer a simple montage of standard information like seen in so many other books on gangs, but a well thought out and methodically paced venture through the annals of the criminal history in the Southern States of the good old U.S.A.

So often in modern culture we tend to associate titles and actions with only media based knowledge. Street Gangs with Los Angeles, Ku Klux Klan with the South, Mobsters with Chicago, and Corruption with Washington D.C. Americans in general suffer from historic amnesia. Either we don't know the past or we ignore the parts that might differ with our current views or beliefs.

Having grown up in the New Orleans area in the 1960's and 70's in a multi-cultural environment I was no stranger to shadier side of the "Big Easy". The historical accuracy of "Dixieland Gangs" almost knocked me down. Names like Carlos Marcello and Carl Douglas "Toehead" White truly took me back in time. It reminded me of how these gangsters were common household names and were spoken in reverence either to their frequent acts of kindness or pure evil.

Gabe Morales has most certainly done his homework. Their ability to demonstrate and remind us of a current, yet often blind, culture of the vast dichotomy of the South and its colorful history of legendary Cops and Robbers is well done. Where else do, you find a Buford Pusser (Walking Tall) or an Alabama Governor willing to declare Martial Law for his own means.

The South has always been the land of Rebels and Rebel Causes. Its vast history of slavery, war, poverty, violence, mayhem, winners, and losers has been a perfect storm for the creation of so many different Criminal Gangs and Anti-Government Extremists. The author accurately describes, in excellent detail, the growth and migration of violent Mid-West Criminal Groups like Gangster Disciples and Latin Kings to the exploitation of major cities throughout the South by the criminal expansion of the Crips and Bloods from the West Coast that still flourishes today.

While I enjoyed "Dixieland Gangs" in its entirety, I especially liked the coverage of the mass migration of Central American and Mexican Gangs into the mostly rural states of the South that continues today.

Having been a major player for decades in the effort to get law enforcement, state, and local governments in the South to recognize the growing threat of these groups I found myself on the phone many times with Gabe Morales who acted as a confidant and adviser. "Dixieland Gangs" demonstrates how a lack of early response to these gangs and often denial by police and community has been very costly and it still prevails to this day. Law enforcement in these areas are always in a stage of playing catch up.

"Dixieland Gangs" is a book for every Concerned Citizen, Gang Officer, Criminal Justice Student, and Academic Historians' shelf in and out of the South.

Again, Well Done!

T. Hunter Glass

Criminal Gang Expert and Consultant

American Civil War and Reconstruction

The Civil War in the United States occurred from 1861 to 1865 to determine the survival of the Union or independence for the Confederacy. Among the 34 states that existed in 1861, seven Southern slave states individually declared their secession from the United States of America and formed the Confederate States of America. The original states were: South Carolina, Georgia, Florida, Alabama, Mississippi, Louisiana, and Texas. After the war started, Virginia, Arkansas, North Carolina, and Tennessee joined them to equal eleven states in all.

The Confederate government, under President Jefferson Davis, was never diplomatically recognized by any foreign country, they were considered renegades, or "Rebels". The states that remained loyal to President Abraham Lincoln were known as the Union or the North. Freed Blacks and slaves fought in the war.

While the war had its origin in the factious issue of slavery, especially the extension of slavery into the western territories, it was much deeper than that. It was a fight for a way of life, one largely rural (the South), and one increasingly urban (the North). After four years of combat, which left up to 750,000 Americans dead, both Union and Confederate, and destroyed much of the South's infrastructure, the Confederacy collapsed and slavery was abolished.

Afterwards, the Reconstruction (1865-1877) period began of restoring national unity and guaranteeing civil rights to freed slaves. But, there are many people even today who say slavery did not end, "it just changed chains".

Angela Davis, an activist and radical in the 1960s with ties to the Black Panther Party and Communist Party U.S.A., noted that throughout the time when slavery was practiced in the U.S., Blacks and Whites were required to break the law to oppose the practice of slavery. Supporters of the Underground Railroad, a network of secret routes and safe houses provided by Abolitionists and allies to enslaved people in the United States acted in "flagrant violation of the fugitive slave law."

Mark Colvin, a Professor at George Mason University, states that in some parts of the southeastern U.S., namely South Carolina, "crime was believed to be perpetrated almost exclusively by Blacks." Punishment, then, was under the almost exclusive control of plantation owners. That behavior was supported by the overwhelmingly high percentage of Blacks among all state's citizens.

In Charleston, Colvin noted, the population of Blacks was about eight times that of Whites. Any White criminals who were identified were whipped, branded, and often forced to out-migrate (move to another state), if they were not executed. They were not encouraged to stay as employment opportunities were limited and the number of available (Black) workers was so high. Civil War researcher Jaron Browne claimed that before slavery was abolished there was no real prison system in the U.S., it was only after the Civil War that "the prison system took hold."

Reconstruction

Historians like Eric Foner and Olivia Mahoney generally consider the Reconstruction Era a failure because the South became quite poverty-stricken, while the politicians in power during the War reestablished dominance through violence, intimidation, and discrimination. The recently freed slaves had limited rights and were excluding from politics via "Jim Crow" Laws. Although changes may have seemed very slow to occur, the Reconstruction of the South came with many drastic changes that took a lot of time to negotiate. The end of slavery also brought major changes to the economy in the southeast U.S.

Foner and Mahoney suggested that the practice of slavery was "simultaneously a system of labor, a form of race relations, and the foundation of a distinctive regional ruling class." To newly freed African-Americans, freedom meant independence from control by a master, and many flaunted their independence. Ownership of dogs, guns, and liquor (previously banned) gave a sense of power and the newly-freed residents often exercised their rights abundantly.

While the nuclear family was often used during slavery to help maintain control, periodically a family member was sold off which caused great pain.

Following emancipation, many freemen made a concerted effort to reunite with family members, and the family unit became a powerful force. Many former slaves claimed joint ownership of the land they worked while enslaved, and some actually seized land as their own without official ownership, taking up residence in a Tennessee plantation owner's home. While many young freed slaves migrated up North, some older ones were too frail and/or afraid to make the trip. Plantation life was all they knew so they stayed working on farms even if as low paid workers under dismal conditions.

KKK Activity During the Reconstructions Era

The name Ku Klux Klan (KKK) probably came from the Greek word kuklos, meaning "circle." Klan was an alliterative version of "clan," thus Ku Klux Klan suggested a circle, or a band of brothers.

By the time the six KKK original members met as a social group in December 1865, the opening phase of Reconstruction was nearly complete. All eleven of the former rebel states had been rebuilt on astonishingly lenient terms which allowed many of the ex-Confederate leaders to return to positions of power. Southern state legislatures began enacting laws which made it clear that the aristocrats who ran them intended to yield none of their pre-war power and dominance over poor Whites and especially over Blacks. These laws, known as the Black Codes (Jim Crow Laws) described earlier, in some cases amounted to a virtual re-enslavement of Blacks.

In Louisiana, the Democratic convention resolved that "we hold this to be a

Government of White People, made and to be perpetuated for the exclusive benefit of the White race, and...that the people of African descent cannot be considered as citizens of the United States." Mississippi and Florida, in particular, enacted vicious Black Codes, other Southern states (except North Carolina) passed somewhat less severe versions. President Andrew Johnson (1865-1869), even though he was Abraham Lincoln's Vice President, did nothing to prevent the Codes from being enforced. Johnson was born in poverty in Raleigh, North Carolina, and prior to his VP appointment, was the only sitting senator from a Confederate state who did not resign his seat upon learning of his state's secession. Johnson had strong ties to the Old South and even opposed the Fourteenth Amendment giving citizenship to ex-slaves.

With the passage of the Military Reconstruction Acts in March 1867, and the prospect of freed men voting in the South, the Klan became more organized. From 1868 through the early 1870s the Ku Klux Klan mostly functioned as a loosely organized group of political and social terrorists. The Klan's goals included the political defeat of Lincoln's Republican Party and the maintenance of absolute White supremacy in response to newly gained civil and political rights by southern Blacks after the war. They were more successful in achieving their political goals than they were with their social goals during this time period.

 **Confederate General Nathan Bedford Forrest**

A legendary Confederate General and former slave trader named Nathan Bedford Forrest was from Tennessee. He joined the Klan fairly soon after it began. The KKK, looking for a worthy leader, allegedly chose Forrest as the Klan's first Grand Wizard. From 1867-68 there is little doubt that he was its chief missionary, traveling over the South, establishing new chapters and quietly advising new members.

The Nashville Klan Convention was called to grapple with their problems by creating a chain of command and deciding just what kind of organization the Klan would be in the future. The meeting gave birth to the official philosophy of White supremacy as the fundamental creed of the Ku Klux Klan.

Throughout the summer of 1867, the Invisible Empire, as the Klan was also called, changed. It ceased clownish antics that had brought laughter during its parades and other public appearances when it first appeared and instead took on the full nature of a secret and powerful force with a sinister purpose.

 **KKK in North Carolina, 1870**

From middle Tennessee, the Klan quickly was established in nearby counties, and soon in North and South Carolina. In some counties the Klan became the de facto law, an invisible government that state officials could not or would not control.

In Georgia conservative Whites, frustrated with their political failures during 1867, began to look for new ways to defeat their Republican enemies and control recently freed Blacks. For many, the KKK and its public political wing, the Young Men's Democratic Clubs, offered a chance to take direct action against "niggers".

In February and March 1868, General Forrest visited Atlanta several times and met with prominent Georgia conservatives. It is believed Forrest helped organize nationwide Klan structures during these visits. By the summer of 1868, the Klan was widespread all across Georgia, then moved into Mississippi and Alabama.

As violence escalated, it turned to general lawlessness, and some Klan groups even began fighting each other. In Nashville, a gang of outlaws who adopted the Klan disguise came to be known as the Black Ku Klux Klan. For several months middle Tennessee was plagued by a guerrilla war between recognized and bogus Klans.

When robed Klansmen were at their peak of power, alarmed Northerners justifiably saw the Klan as an attempt of unrepentant Confederates to win back through terrorism what they had been unable to obtain on the battlefield. Such a simple view did not totally explain the Klan's sway over the South, but there is little doubt that many a Confederate veteran exchanged his rebel gray for the hoods and sheets of the Invisible Empire. Their exact numbers are unknown, but it is believed by many historians that they were several thousand strong by 1868.

Finally, and most importantly, there were the dire conditions many Southerners were faced with immediately after the war. Their cities, plantations and farms were ruined; they were impoverished and often hungry; there was an occupation Union army in their midst in old Dixie; and Reconstruction governments threatened to usurp the traditional White ruling authority. In the first few months after the fighting ended, White Southerners had to contend with losses of life, liberty, property and, in their eyes, most of all their honor.

Soon, the Klan became under increased attack by Congress and the Reconstruction state governments. The leaders of the Klan thus realized that the Invisible Empire's end was at hand, at least as any sort of real organized force.

It is widely believed that Forrest ordered the Klan to disband in January 1869, but the surviving document is rather ambiguous. Some historians think Forrest's "order" was just a trick so he could deny any future responsibility or publically disavow direct knowledge of Klan atrocities. Others say it was just a smart business move so he could get approval for his private railroad ventures.

Whatever the actual date, it is clear that as an organized, cohesive body across the South, the Ku Klux Klan had ceased to exist by the end of 1871. Forrest testified before a Congressional investigation on Klan activities on June 27, 1871. Forrest denied membership, but his individual role in the KKK was beyond the scope of the investigating committee. Some said he had a change of heart, others doubted it.

The frequency of late 19th/early 20th century lynch mobs in the South which, while not organized gangs, nevertheless displayed episodes of mass organized violence.

The Klan would not be heard from again until "The Birth of a Nation" (1915).

Republican and Democratic Parties

From 1880 to the early 1960s, White populists of the Deep South regained control of state governments and overwhelmingly identified as and supported the Democratic Party, mostly in opposition to "Lincoln's Republican Party". Many in the South belonged to the Democratic Party's moderate-to-conservative wing. At the same time, numerous Republicans continued to be elected in local offices through the 1880s and into the 1890s. The Republicans and Populists (1891-1908) briefly elected governors in some states, as well as other fusion candidates. The Republicans elected an African-American congressman as late as 1894.

The Black Codes

During the Reconstruction Era, as conservative Democratic Whites took back power, former slaves were stifled by so-called "Black Codes". According to Angela Davis, these rules prohibited social discourse between Blacks and Whites and gave extensive control over the lives of Black employees by White employers.

The Black Codes prohibited former slaves from contributions to society and the justice system as serving on jury duty, carrying weapons, and violating curfew. The Black Codes criminalized otherwise legal activity, such as standing around in a certain area of town or walking in an area at night. Those activities became known as loitering and breaking curfew. Resistance to such laws occurred, which resulted in many Blacks being jailed. It was also often used as an excuse to jail somebody even if no violation existed. Davis found that many Blacks armed themselves in groups, and "protect themselves from White terrorists who were, in turn, protected by law enforcement agencies, if not actually identified with them."

As a result of Black Code violations, the percentage of African-Americans in Deep South prisons grew exponentially. Reconstruction governments ultimately defeated the Black Codes. In their absence, some Southern politicians implemented vagrancy laws that were so broad they allowed for the arrest of "almost any unemployed person." Colvin found that new statutes prohibited Blacks from employment in law enforcement, or serving as a judge or on a jury. Following the adoption of the new penalties, the number of convicts incarcerated increased dramatically in at least two states from 1874-1877:

- 272-1,072 in Mississippi
- 432-1,441 in Georgia

Convict Leasing

Shortly after the Black Codes were defeated, a system of convict leasing was devised to let wealthy landowners "lease" cheap labor by prisoners from the state. According to Browne, "in 1878, Georgia leased out 1,239 prisoners, and all but 115 were African-Americans." Colvin suggests the expansion of convict leasing (to all former Confederate states) was partly driven by the need for forced, cheap labor and state revenue. The railroads, as well as lumber, iron, and coal mills, and many manufacturing facilities often used convict leasing as a primary labor option.

Chain Gangs

Convict leasing ultimately fell out of favor and the concept of the chain gang began. The primary function was to assist with large road development projects. Prisoners were shackled together while they worked outside the prison walls.

"I Am a Fugitive from a Georgia Chain Gang!" is a book written by Robert Elliott Burns in 1932. The book tells the story of Burns' imprisonment on a chain gang in Georgia in the 1920s, his subsequent escape, and the furor that developed afterwards. The story was first published in January 1932, serialized in True Detective Mysteries magazine. Later that year, Burns' story was made into the motion picture starring Paul Muni. The book and movie were both credited with helping to reform deplorable conditions on Deep South chain gangs, by Georgia Governor Ellis Arnall in 1943.

Freedom and the Move to the City

The economic growth that came as a result of increased manufacturing in the North and cities like St. Louis and New Orleans caused an increase in migration from the South. Young Black males found opportunities for freedom and wages were usually greater than in towns and cities in rural areas. Many of those who migrated to the cities in the 1880s found that access to such benefits as literacy, property and land ownership, and education increased. Colvin noted that many joined organizations designed to ensure the indignant mistreatment would never reoccur.

Professor Colvin believed the increased migration of Black men also loosened their social bonds, making them more susceptible to the temptation to commit crime in order to improve their status and condition. Materialism was a goal many aspired to. Increased criminal activity led to an increased number of police encounters, which led to increases in incarceration rates, which led to more stereotypes.

Crime rose in the region in the late 1880s and early 1890s. Whites typically held Blacks responsible for the increase in the crime rate. Southern newspapers publicized Black crime and exaggerated its impact. Black males were often depicted as drunk, high, and sex crazed.

Many people today believe these stereotypes still exist.

Gangs in the North

According to Belgium author Luc Sante in his book "Low Life: Lures and Snares of Old New York", the first street gangs in the U.S. appeared around 1783, at the end of the American Revolution. These gangs emerged in the eastern U.S. cities, which had conditions conducive to formation and growth, mostly created by the many waves of immigration and urban overcrowding.

The first criminal gang with a definite acknowledged leadership, the Forty Thieves, formed around 1826 in the Five Points area of New York. They had a younger faction called the Little Forty Thieves. The second recorded gang, the Kerryonians, was named after a county in Ireland from which they came. Similar gangs with interesting names also formed in Five Points, including the Chichesters, Roach Guards, Plug Uglies (named after their large plug hats), Shirt Tails (distinguished by wearing their shirts outside their trousers), and Dead Rabbits.

In both New York and Chicago, the earliest gangs formed in concert with the arrival of predominantly white European immigrants from 1783 to 1860 period (particularly German, French, British, and Scandinavians). Useni Perkins, author of "The Explosion of Chicago's Black Street Gangs-1900 to Present" found that White street gangs had been documented in Chicago since the 1860s. Other groups, including Irish, Italians, Jews, and Poles, arrived in large numbers from 1880 to 1920. The early street gangs of New York and Chicago were almost exclusively made up of immigrants. The second-generation youth of these ethnic groups were most susceptible to gang involvement.

By the 1880s, Irish gangs like the Dukies and the Shielders influenced activity around the Chicago Stockyards by robbing men leaving work, and terrorizing the other immigrants. The European-American gangs fought constantly among themselves, but sometimes joined together to war against Black gangs who arrived from the southern states after the Civil War.

The Role of Assimilation

Assimilation has been seen in the past by many as an American tradition. It was viewed as a process immigrants should strive for to become part of their new culture, community, and country. The theory of assimilation is a process that brings ethnic minorities into the mainstream of American life. It is a gradual process for some, others adapt quite rapidly, especially those seeking greater success in American society and business.

Of course, some people, especially Nationalist and Separatists, do not think it is such a good thing to assimilate.

The process of assimilation often involves shifts as a change in attire, living arrangements, food preferences, music, and language. American sociologists Richard D. Alba and Victor Nee identified a scale that indicated the degree of expected simplicity with which a group could be expected to assimilate in the U.S. The scale ranged from English-speaking (White) Protestants at the top to African-Americans at the bottom. Those at the top could expect a problem-free and short process, while those in the middle, like those from the Mediterranean area of Europe (Italy) would experience a moderately long and arduous process of up to six generations. Those in the non-European groups, especially those of darker complexion who were, therefore, closer to the bottom, could expect a problem-laden process that could continue "into the indefinite future."

One could argue even without looking at these statistics, there is bias in America.

The racial diversity of Hispanics, including Mexicans,, causes a mix of issues when this scale is applied, although society members often find other distinguishers besides race, like language, culture, and musical preference, to evaluate assimilation.

In particular, many Hispanics came from countries located close to the border. Many go back and forth to these home countries and the U.S. This happens far more frequently on average than to non-Hispanic immigrants. Some Hispanics, Mexicans and Puerto Ricans in particular, argue that "they didn't cross the border, the border crossed them".

Formal agreements, such as the Treaty of Guadalupe Hidalgo, signed between the United States and other countries often guaranteed certain rights, but as many Hispanics point out with treaties that were signed with Native Americans, these were quickly broken.

Border security, legal status of immigrants, and American assimilation were big issue in the hotly contested 2016 Presidential election. Republican candidate Donald Trump was for a "Deportation Force" and building a wall. Democratic candidate Hilary Clinton actually voted for the building of a "fence and wall", but offered Amnesty instead of Deportation for millions already in the U.S.

Again, the theory of assimilation occurs when people are motivated to make the changes necessary to embrace their new country and the culture into which they are attempting to assimilate accepts them and their efforts. The process is stifled if either component is not present. Assimilation into mainstream society requires a combination of social, financial, and human capital investments both within and external to the ethnic networks that form when a sizeable group enters a new society.

Studies have shown that because of the successful assimilation of early European immigrant groups into American society, gangs in those societies virtually disappeared by the third generation. A notable exception would be the existence today after several generations of La Cosa Nostra that still has direct ties to Sicily.

That has not been the case with Mexican Americans who may not show assimilation until the fourth generation at the earliest. It also does not take into account the theory of "institutional racism".

Institutional racism was defined by Sir William Macpherson in the 1999 Lawrence report (UK) as: "The collective failure of an organization to provide an appropriate and professional service to people because of their color, culture, or ethnic origin. It can be seen or detected in processes, attitudes and behavior which amount to discrimination through unwitting prejudice, ignorance, thoughtlessness and racist stereotyping which disadvantage minority ethnic people."

Author Gabe Morales' experience is some gradual assimilation happens with most Latinos, it just happens slower usually than other groups, in great part to the factors listed previously. One could also argue that the Hispanic influence on American culture is often greater than any other culture except the English.

Those who have studied the phenomenon of assimilation speculate that it may be attributed to educational or economic attainment. As some have found, such as Edward M. Telles, Vilma Ortiz, Joan W. Moore in their book "Generations of Exclusion: Mexican-Americans, Assimilation, and Race" (2009), "Low educational status is the main reason for low job status."

Indeed, Gabe Morales' experience is one of the biggest factors of youth joining a gang or become incarcerated, is often directly related to their educational level.

Unlike African Americans, Mexican Americans do not usually have to add labor market discrimination (hiring bias) to the list of hurdles to employment. Many companies like to hire them, but some Blacks in the U.S. do resent them "taking their jobs" even more than many White workers which can lead to "Black vs. Brown" violence in some places in the U.S.

Scholars such as Telles, Ortiz, and Moore observed that Mexicans experienced bias in the U.S., albeit in a different way than did African-Americans. The scientifically-endorsed theories of race encouraged White citizens to alienate and subordinate Mexicans in the southern U.S. at every opportunity. Based on historical events, specifically the Mexican-American War and the Battle of the Alamo, many Whites also held a high degree of animosity for Mexicans. Political and immigration tensions in cities like Phoenix, AZ, and controversies surrounding the "Toughest Sheriff in America", ex-Maricopa County (Phoenix) Sheriff Joe Arpio, are an example of White anger towards Mexicans even today.

Mexicans were geographically segregated, much like Blacks, until the 1950s.

Rarely do immigrants with gang affiliation arrive in a new country, but this can happen sometimes with Latinos coming into the U.S.

 **Mara Salvatrucha**

Central Americans gangs like Mara Salvatrucha or Barrio 18 originated in Los Angeles, and later exported to Central America; some who joined there have illegally immigrated into the United States.

Gang affiliation may occur in the second and subsequent generations, in response to a number of environmental factors, not the least of which is the marginalization and bias associated with some societies. With each generation, familiarity with and often engagement in the gang lifestyle increased and thus gang involvement grew, often through the fourth generation. Gang involvement was seen more often in the members of the society who were born in the U.S.

We will address issues surrounding Mexicans/Hispanics and gangs in more depth in Chapter 4.

Sources (By Author):

An updated history of the new Afrikan prison struggle. Acoli, S., James, J., 2003

Remaking the American mainstream: Assimilation and Contemporary Immigration, Harvard University Press, Alba, R. and Nee, V., 2003

Radicalized identities and the formation of black gangs in Los Angeles. Urban Geography, Alex A. Alonso, 2004

The Promise Of The New South: Life after Reconstruction, New York, NY: Oxford University Press, Ayers, E.L., 1992

The Ghettoization of Blacks in Los Angeles: The emergence of street gangs. Journal of African-American Studies, Brown, G.C., Vigil, J.D., and Taylor, E.R., 2012

Sheriff Joe Arpaio to face criminal charges over immigration, CBS, 10/11/16

Penitentiaries, reformatories, and chain gangs: Social theory and the history of punishment in nineteenth century America. New York, NY: St. Martin's Press, Colvin, M., 1997

Something wicked this way comes: A historical account of Black gangsterism offers wisdom and warning for African-American leadership. Journal of Black Studies, Cureton, S.R., 2009

Imprisoned Intellectuals: America's political prisoners write on life, liberation, and rebellion. New York, NY: Rowan and Littlefield, Angela Y. Davis, 1971

America's reconstruction: People and politics after the Civil War. Baton Rouge, LA: Louisiana State University Press, Foner, E. and Mahoney, O., 1995

Ku-Klux: The Birth of the Klan During Reconstruction, Elaine Frantz Parsons, 2016

Ku Klux Klan in the Reconstruction Era, Georgia Southern University, 10/03/02

Street Gangs: Yesterday and Today. Wayne, PA: Hastings Books, Haskins, J.,1974

Reconstruction. History Past and Perspective. The New American, WP Hoar, 4/6/15

Low life: Lures and snares of old New York: Vintage Books; Howell, J.C., 2012

Political prisoners, prisons, and Black liberation. Joy James, 2003

Imprisoned Intellectuals: America's political prisoners write on life, liberation, and rebellion. New York, NY: Rowan and Littlefield, Joy James, 2003

Violence by youth gangs and youth groups as a crime problem in major American cities. Washington, D.C., U.S. Department of Justice, Miller, W.B., 1975

Understanding youth street gangs: Economic restructuring and the urban underclass. JAI Press, Joan W. Moore, 1998

Chicano Gangs and the History of the Southwest, CJS, G.Morales, S.Lucero, 2014

Explosion of Chicago's black street gangs: 1900 to present, Third World Press, Perkins, U.E., 1987

Gangs in American Communities. Thousand Oaks, CA: SAGE Publications, Santa, L., 1991

Ku Klux Klan, A History of Racism and Violence, Southern Poverty Law Center, 2011

Generations of exclusion. New York, NY: Russell Sage Foundation, Telles, E.E. & Ortiz, V., 2008

The Gangs: A study of 1,313 gangs in Chicago, New Chicago School Press, Thrasher, F.M., 1927, Reprinted 2000

WWI, Prohibition, and the World War II Era

The Birth of a Nation (originally called The Clansman) is a 1915 American silent epic drama film directed and co-produced by D.W. Griffith and starring Lillian Gish. The screenplay was adapted from a novel, The Clansman, written by Thomas Dixon Jr. while Griffith co-wrote the screenplay with Frank E. Woods, and co-produced the film with Harry Aitken. It was released on February 8, 1915.

The film's release is credited as being one of the events that inspired the formation of the "second era" Ku Klux Klan at Stone Mountain, Georgia, in the same year. The Birth of a Nation, along with the trial and lynching of Leo Frank for the 1913 murder of Mary Phagan in Atlanta, was used as a recruiting tool for the KKK.

This second wave revival of the KKK began just after World War I (1914) started. When American fighting men came home after the war in 1918, many of them did not like Blacks taking jobs they thought should go to White men.

The second Klan wave flourished nationwide in the early to mid-1920s, particularly in urban areas of the Midwest and West. It was rooted in Protestant communities, opposed Jews, as well as the Catholic Church. This second wave adopted a standard white costume and used similar code words as the first Klan, while adding cross burnings and mass KKK parades to intimidate Blacks. Many law enforcement in southern states were members, if not KKK sympathizers.

Some people believe that, at its height in 1925, the Klan had 4 million members.

A big part of this growth was in big cities in the Midwest and West. On August 8, 1925, an estimated 40,000 KKK marched down Pennsylvania Avenue in Washington D.C. right front of the White House which showed how powerful they were. Some Whites in the South felt they needed to join the KKK and other groups to protect what their Southern ancestors fought and died for in the battlefield. Many Blacks in the South felt disappointed at this regrowth of the KKK and continually disenfranchised from the American political and economic system.

This was a big factor why many young Blacks in the early 1900s joined street gangs and this disenfranchisement continues to be a factor today.

Community Transitional Stages

Black history expert Steven R. Cureton observed that the existence of Black street gangs in urban cities evolved from four Community Transitional Stages: Defined Community (Stage 1: 1920 to 1929), Community Conversion (Stage 2: 1930 to 1965), Gangster Colonization (Stage 3: 1966 to 1989), and Gangster Politicization (Stage 4: 1990 to 2000).

Defined Community (Stage 1: 1920 to 1929)

In the Defined Community stage, the mass migration of Southern Blacks put the new arrivals in cities near all White neighborhoods. This sparked interracial conflict and some Whites moved away as moor Blacks poured in. Some powerbrokers participated in community covenants, which they used to effectively ban African-Americans from establishing residency in certain neighborhoods. White male youth groups (gangs) formed and violently resisted attempts at racial integration in the neighborhoods, which led to Black brotherhoods also evolving into social protection groups and later violent criminal activities (gangs).

Community Conversion (Stage 2: 1930 to 1965)

During the stage known as Community Conversion, the Great Depression (1930 to early 1940s) and the Civil Rights Movement (1955 to 1965) produced a poor underclass. The Great Depression crippled the economic foundation of the Black community severely, many Black owned businesses went out of business and never recovered. The Civil Rights Movement was more beneficial to a select group of better educated, professional, and vocationally skilled Blacks. Prior to the 1940s, much of the crime in Black communities was controlled by White gangsters and organized crime. Occasionally, a Black gangster like "Casper" Holstein or "Madame" Stephanie Saint-Clair was able to run numbers rackets in places like Harlem, NYC, but often did so by paying protection or a tax to White gangsters.

Gangster Colonization (Stage 3: 1966 to 1989)

This stage is when modern street gangs gained a foothold in the social fabric of the urban underclass. Marginalized residents (mostly young males, usually Black or Hispanic) wanted access to the opportunities offered by society, so they traded in drugs, guns, stolen goods, prostitutes, and gambling to make their living. Respect governed street interactions and affected individual chances of survival. Sadly, respect was often earned and maintained by engaging in violence, even murder.

Gangster Politicization (Stage 4: 1990 to 2000 and Present).

During the Gangster Politicization period (1990 to 2000) neighborhoods often became vast ganglands. These areas were socially organized around typical male rites of passage (from boyhood to manhood or baby gangster to original gangster) and normative expectations (i.e., street protocol, dealing with enemies, the value of gang alliances, seizing control of turf, drug and gun distribution, recreation, etc.).

Author Steve R. Cureton, Ph.D., found that during this period, the gang became further embedded in the fabric of the underclass Black community as each generation of potential young male gangbangers needed a street education to become better gangbangers. Older gangsters assumed the responsibility of passing on knowledge of gangster history, protocol, and politics. They became known as the OG's (Original Gangsters) who often served as advisors to younger ones.

Many former gang members eventually became involved in community activist groups during the late 1960s through mid-70s as well as after the Rodney King Riots (1992). The current "Black Lives Matter" Movement would be an example of some gang members joining protests against police and the system. Riots in Ferguson, Baltimore, and North Carolina often involved older gang members as protest organizers and agitators as well as involving younger looters.

Of course Blacks were not the only ones involved in politics, prohibition, or crime.

Some of the most notorious White gangsters of the Prohibition Era had ties to the southeastern portion of the United States.

Charles "Pretty Boy" Floyd

Charles "Pretty Boy" Floyd (1904-1934) has remained an infamous character in American folklore, often typecast as a hardened crook yet frequently referred to as a Midwestern Robin Hood, a victim of poverty and circumstance led to a life of crime. He committed robberies in Northwest Arkansas in the 1930s. Floyd lived fast in his twenties and died fast on July 23, 1934, at the young age of thirty.

The Ma Barker Gang, named after Kate "Ma" Barker, operated during the Great Depression (1929-late 1930s). FBI agents discovered the hideout of "Ma" Barker and her son, Fred, after Arthur "Doc" Barker was arrested in Chicago on January 8, 1935. On the morning of January 16, 1935, FBI agents ordered the gang to surrender at Lake Weir, Florida. Fred Barker opened fire; both he and his mother were killed by federal agents after an intense, hours-long shootout. Allegedly, locals came out to watch the raid unfolding, even holding picnics during gunfire.

The gang's leader, Alvin "Creepy" Karpis, and other Barker gang members left three days before the shootout so they escaped death. Karpis was another criminal who enjoyed spending time and money in Hot Springs, Arkansas. Before their capture in Malvern, Arkansas, Karpis and his accomplice Fred Hunter stayed at two different cottages on Lake Catherine and Lake Hamilton, located about 60 miles southwest of Little Rock, in the later part of 1935 and early 1936. Karpis and Hunter moved frequently in the Hot Springs resort area as they knew the FBI and U.S. postal investigators were looking locally for clues to their whereabouts.

Karpis life was rare for a gangster, after serving time at Alcatraz Prison from 1936-62, he was moved to McNeil Island Prison in Washington State until 1969 when he was deported to his home country of Canada. He died in 1979 in Spain at age 72.

Bonnie and Clyde

Arkansas was also frequented often by Bonnie Parker, Clyde Barrow, and their associates, collectively known as the "Barrow Gang", between 1932 and 1934. The gang's criminal exploits in Arkansas included murder, attempted murder, kidnapping, robbery, and automobile theft. Western Arkansas, including Ozarks Hillbilly friends, was part of the circuit of back roads that Clyde Barrow used to evade lawmen from other states. The most serious crime committed in the state by the Barrow Gang was the murder of Marshal Henry D. Humphrey of Alma, AR, while the gang was hiding out in a tourist camp in Fort Smith, AR, in June 1933.

Frank "Jelly" Nash was often referred to as "the most successful bank robber in U.S. history". He spent part of his childhood in Paragould, Arkansas, and was arrested in Hot Springs the day before his death. On June 15, 1933, two FBI agents traveled to Hot Springs after learning Nash could frequently be found in town at the White Front Cigar Store. After being arrested and placed in transport to Kansas City, Missouri, Nash was shot and killed at the Kansas City Union Station during in a botched rescue attempt by armed thugs loyal to Nash.

Another famous gangster who had ties to the South was Charles "Lucky" Luciano. Luciano was born in Sicily but made his bones in New York City. Luciano is considered the father of modern organized crime in the U.S. for his establishment of the first "Commission". Luciano, along with his associate Meyer Lansky, was instrumental in the development of the La Cosa Nostra crime syndicate in the U.S.

On April 1, 1936, a New York detective on assignment spotted Luciano, a well-known pimp, strolling along Bathhouse Row in Hot Springs, AR, along with the city's Chief of Detectives. The New York detective approached Luciano and invited Luciano to return with him peacefully to the Big Apple where Luciano would be placed under arrest. Luciano naturally declined, saying he was having a good time gambling and cavorting in the "Spa City" which at the time was politically corrupt and a safe haven for criminals. Luciano was detained anyway and moved to confinement in Little Rock the next day. Later, in June of the same year, Luciano was sentenced to thirty to fifty years at the maximum security Dannemora Prison in New York for compulsory prostitution (pimping by force).

The safe, secluded, and scenic location of Hot Springs also made it an ideal hideout for Chicago's Al "Scarface" Capone, who made the resort area one of his preferred getaways. Capone would rent out entire floors of Hot Springs hotels for himself and his entourage. Local political and legal corruption made it a gambler's paradise long before Las Vegas made its mark on society. Though illegal, and a felony under Arkansas law, gambling was no secret to the majority of local authorities. Police officers, judges, and even the mayor turned a blind eye to the industry and to high-rolling gangsters who enjoyed partaking in local vices.

Owen "Owney" Madden, often referred to as "The English Godfather" and "The Killer", came to Hot Springs in 1935, seeking a quieter slower-paced Arkansas life as opposed to the constant violence and fast life of New York City. Originally from England, Madden grew up in the tough neighborhoods of Manhattan's "Hell's Kitchen" and is best known for giving more "organization" to organized crime as depicted in the movie "The Cotton Club".

He also often advised Luciano who took organization a step further.

A respected and well-liked man amongst his hardened circle of peers, Madden settled into Hot Springs with ease. As time passed, more and more of Owney's old criminal colleagues arrived. The word spread that Hot Springs was the perfect hideout for criminals running from police investigations, so they came in droves.

He lived in Hot Springs until his death in 1965.

One of his frequent contacts was a local madam.

 **Maxine Temple Jones**

Maxine Temple Jones was a Hot Springs businesswoman during the period from 1945 to the early 1970s. A well-known madam with numerous political connections, she managed a lucrative brothel operation that catered to politicians, businessmen, and mobsters. Jones was able to expand her business, most notably with the purchase of a large home on Palm Street which became known as "The Mansion" thanks to her top-tier connections. She provided her "high-classed" clientele with years of illegal adult entertainment before "going straight" and publishing a tell-all autobiography "Call Me Madam" in 1983.

New Orleans Crime Family

The Matranga Crime Family was established by Charles and Antonio (Tony) Matranga in the late 1800s making it one of the earliest recorded American Mafia crime families. They operated in the "Big Easy", as New Orleans was often called, during the late 19th century until the beginning of Prohibition in 1920.

Born in Sicily, Carlo and Antonio Matranga settled in New Orleans during the 1870s where they eventually opened a saloon and brothel. Using their business as a base of operations, the Matranga brothers began establishing lucrative organized criminal activities including extortion and labor racketeering. Receiving tribute payments from Italian laborers and dockworkers, as well as from the rival Provenzano crime family that held a near monopoly of commercial shipping from South American fruit shipments, they eventually began moving in on the Provenzano's fruit loading operations intimidating them with threats of violence.

Some say they introduced "The Black Hand" to America by leaving extortion note threats signed with a black ink palm print. Bad things happened to refusals.

Although the Provenzanos withdrew in favor of giving the Matrangas a cut of waterfront racketeering by the late 1880s, the two families eventually went to war over the grocery and produce businesses held by the Provenzanos. As both sides employed a large number of Mafiosi from their native Monreale, Sicily, the violent gang war began attracting police attention, particularly from New Orleans Police Chief David Hennessy who began investigating into the warring organizations.

Within months of his investigation, Hennessy was shot and killed by several unidentified attackers while walking home on the night of October 15, 1890.

The murder of Hennessey created a huge backlash from the city and, although Charles and several members of the Matrangas were arrested, they were eventually tried and acquitted in February 1891 with Charles and a 14-year-old member acquitted midway through the trial as well as four more who were eventually acquitted and three others released in hung juries. The decision caused strong protests from residents, angered by the controversy surrounding the case (particularly in the face of incriminating evidence and jury tampering), and the following month a lynch mob stormed the jail hanging 11 of the 17 Matranga members still waiting to be brought to trial including Antonio Bagnetto, Bastiano Incardona, Antonio Marchese, Pietro Monastero, and Manuel Politzi.

It was the largest lynching in American history. The lynch mob was estimated to be over 3000 and it included both rich and poor. It was said that many of the mob were wealthy but had been victims of extortion by the Mafia over the years. Many of the poor had been victims of violence and abuse by the Mafia. It should be noted that all of these lynchers were White and their victims were all White (Italian). Vigilante justice in those days was often taken regardless of color.

The Hennessey lynchings led to the American Mafia adopting a hard and fast rule that policemen and other law enforcement officials were not to be harmed.

Matranga was able to escape from the lynch mob and, upon returning to New Orleans, resumed his position as head of the New Orleans crime family eventually forcing the declining Provenzanos out by the end of the decade. Matranga would rule over the New Orleans underworld until shortly after Prohibition when he turned over leadership over to "Silver Dollar Sam" Carollo in the early 1920s.

Born in Sicily, Sylvestro Carolla immigrated to the United States with his parents in 1904. By 1918, Carolla had become a high-ranking member of Matranga's organization, eventually succeeding him following Matranga's retirement in 1922. After assuming control of Matranga's minor bootlegging operations, Carolla waged a full-fledged war against rival bootlegging gangs, gaining full control following a personal murder he committed of his last rival, William Bailey, in December 1930.

Gaining considerable political influence within New Orleans, Carolla is said to have used his powerful connections when, in 1929, Al Capone supposedly traveled to the city demanding Carolla supply the Chicago Outfit rather than Chicago's Sicilian boss Joe Aiello with imported alcohol from docks of the Big Easy. Meeting Capone as he arrived at a New Orleans train station, Carolla allegedly accompanied police officers who reportedly disarmed Capone's bodyguards and broke their fingers, then forced Capone to return to Chicago.

In 1930, Carolla was arrested for the shooting of federal narcotics agent Cecil Moore, which took place during an undercover drug buy. Despite support by several allied New Orleans police officers who testified Carolla was in New York at the time of the murder, he was sentenced to two years.

Released in 1934, Carolla negotiated a deal with New York mobsters Frank Costello and Phillip "Dandy Phil" Kastel, as well as infamous Louisiana Senator Huey "Kingfish" Long, to bring slot machines into Louisiana following New York Mayor Fiorello LaGuardia's attacks on organized crime. Carolla, with his lieutenant Carlos Marcello, ran illegal gambling operations undisturbed for years.

Carolla's immigration status problems continued. He was scheduled to be deported in 1940, after serving two years in Atlanta Federal Penitentiary, following his arrest on a narcotics charge in 1938. His deportation was delayed following the U.S. entry into World War II and Carolla continued to control New Orleans crime.

Then a media campaign, begun by reporter Drew Pearson, exposed an attempt by Congressman Jimmy Morrison to pass a bill awarding Carolla with American citizenship (thereby making his deportation illegal).

Carolla was finally deported in April 1947.

Soon after returning to Sicily, Carolla organized a partnership with fellow exile Charles "Lucky" Luciano, establishing criminal enterprises in Mexico. Briefly returning to the United States in 1949, Carolla was deported again the following year as control of the New Orleans crime family reverted to Carlos Marcello.

Born Calogero Minacore to Sicilian parents, Carlos Marcello was brought to the United States in 1911 and his family settled in a decaying plantation house near Metairie, Louisiana. As a teen Marcello turned to petty crime in the French Quarter, which was then considered New Orleans' "Little Italy". He was imprisoned for leading a crew of teenage gangsters who carried out armed robberies in the small towns near New Orleans. These charges were later allegedly dropped, but the following year he was convicted of assault and robbery, and was sentenced to the state penitentiary for nine years, eventually serving five.

In 1938, Marcello was arrested and charged with the sale of more than 10 kilos of marijuana. Despite receiving another lengthy prison sentence and a $76,830 fine, Marcello served less than 10 months in prison. Many New Orleans residents believe this was due to Marcello's heavy influence on the criminal justice system with likely payoffs. On his release from prison, Marcello became associated with Frank Costello, leader of the Genovese Crime Family in New York.

By the end of 1947, Marcello took control of Louisiana's gambling network. He also joined forces with Meyer Lansky in order to take over and split the profits from some of the most important gambling casinos in the New Orleans area. According to former members of the Chicago Outfit, Marcello was also assigned a cut of the money skimmed from Las Vegas casinos in exchange for providing muscle in Florida real estate deals. By this time, Marcello had been crowned as the "Godfather of the Mafia" in New Orleans by the family's capos and the Commission. He was to hold this position for the next 30 years.

Carlos "Mr. New Orleans" Marcello-U.S. Senate Hearings

On March 24, 1959, Marcello appeared before the Senate Committee investigating organized crime. Serving as chief counsel to the committee was Robert F. Kennedy; his brother, Senator John F. Kennedy (JFK), was a member of the committee. In response to committee questioning, Marcello again invoked the Fifth Amendment by refusing to answer any questions relating to his background, activities, and associates.

In March 1961, Attorney General Kennedy took steps to have Marcello deported to Guatemala (the country Marcello had falsely listed as his birthplace). On April 4, 1961, Marcello was arrested by the authorities and taken forcibly to Guatemala, and left in a remote rural area. Marcello and one of his associates narrowly escaped being murdered by two South American men for what little money they had allegedly guiding them back to a city, where they could return to the United States.

Marcello soon returned the United States.

Undercover informants reported that he made several threats against the Kennedys.

In September 1962, he told private investigator Edward Becker that "a dog will continue to bite you if you cut off its tail (meaning Attorney General Robert Kennedy). Whereas if you cut off the dog's head (meaning President Kennedy), it would cease to cause trouble." Becker reported Marcello, "clearly stated that he was going to arrange to have President Kennedy killed in some way." Marcello told another informant that he would need to take out "insurance" for the assassination by "setting up some nut to take the fall for the job, just like they do in Sicily." Some say that fall guy was Lee Harvey Oswald, a former Marine sharp shooter who defected to the Soviet Union in 1959 and lived there as an expatriate before returning to the U.S. in 1962 before being blamed for the death of John.

Just before JFK was assassinated on November 22, 1963, Jack Ruby made contact with Marcello. Ruby was a known associate of the Marcello family, who operated a strip club in Dallas. There was evidence given to the Warren Commission that Ruby had been involved in the typical underworld activities of gambling, narcotics, and prostitution. After the assassination of Kennedy the FBI investigated Marcello and eventually came to the conclusion that he was not involved in the plot. On the other hand, they also said that they "did not believe Carlos Marcello was a significant organized crime figure" and assessed he earned his living "as a tomato salesman and real estate investor" which caused more rumors to circulate.

As a result of their investigation, the Warren Commission finally concluded there was no direct link between Ruby and Marcello and the Kennedy Assassination.

In 1966 Marcello was arrested in New York City after having met with the National Commission. The meeting was reportedly called because Marcello's leadership was being challenged by Tampa, FL, Mafia boss Santo Trafficante, Jr. and Anthony Carollo, the son of Marcello's predecessor. The Commission reportedly ruled in Marcello's favor just before the police burst in.

Marcello was then charged with consorting with known felons and after a long drawn out legal battle he was eventually convicted of assaulting an FBI agent whom he had punched in the face on his return to Louisiana. Sentenced to two years in prison, he served less than six months, and was released March 1971.

In 1989, he was released after a conviction on bribery charges was overturned. Marcello died in one of his mansions in Metairie, Louisiana, on March 3, 1993 as a free man, and today the Marcello family and descendants still own or control a significant amount of real estate in southeast Louisiana.

The Dixie Mafia

The Dixie Mafia is a criminal organization based in Biloxi, Mississippi, which operates primarily in the Southern United States, hence the name "Dixie". Over the years, the group has used each member's talents in various crime categories to help them move stolen merchandise, illegal alcohol, and illegal drugs. They are also particularly well known for using violence.

Beginning in the late 1960s, the Dixie Mafia began working as a loosely knit group of traveling criminals performing residential burglary, robbery and theft. The gang did not initially function with a set chain of command, but was led by whoever had the most money. Despite the informal structure, the Dixie Mafia had one rule that members were expected to obey: "Thou shalt not snitch to the cops".

Unlike members of the Sicilian Mafia, members of the Dixie Mafia were not connected by family or country of origin. In fact, many of them say the cops invented their name as an excuse to lock them up. They were loosely connected individuals of many nationalities with a common goal in mind: to make money and wield control over illegal moneymaking operations by any means, including influence peddling, bribery of public officials, and even murder.

The gang became known for carrying out contract killings, particularly against former members. During its peak, from the early 1970s to the late 1980s, dozens were murdered (usually shot) by fellow members. Victims were most often killed because they testified, or threatened to testify, against Dixie Mafia. A contract killer William "Blue Eyes" Miller was said to have carried out many of the deaths but this could never be proven in court due to lack of evidence.

"The Strip" in Biloxi, Mississippi, was considered home base for the gang. Mike Gillich, Jr. was the group's unofficial, but de facto kingpin. Gillich was of Croatian descent and from a large, poor family. He raised himself in the city's Point Cadet section to become a wealthy entrepreneur along "The Strip". He eventually owned a string of motels, a bingo parlor, and nightclubs that doubled as strip joints and gambling dens. Gillich was also patron and protector of Kirksey McCord Nix, Jr.

Already one of the gang's most notable members at the age of 22, in December 1965, Nix was caught carrying illegal automatic weapons in Ft. Smith, Arkansas. An old friend of his, Juanda Jones, ran a bordello there. Nix became involved with Jones' adolescent daughter, Sheri LaRa. In later years, she would play a key role in his operations, including direct ties to the murders of Circuit Court Judge Vincent Sherry and his wife, Margaret, a former Biloxi councilwoman and mayoral candidate.

Shortly after Dixie Mafia leader Jeffrey Carter's release from the Louisiana State Penitentiary, Federal authorities were involved in an airplane chase over the Gulf of Mexico after authorities spotted a low flying Piper Cub flying at full speed just a few hundred yards off shore. The pilot of this aircraft ignored Federal authorities attempt to communicate and made a dangerous belly landing just yards away from the shore. He was seen swimming to shore by authorities using infrared night vision. Despite all efforts to have law enforcement on the ground to locate this pilot, he was never caught. The airplane was later determined to be stolen, and there was nothing illegal on board. However, law enforcement authorities believe that this low flying pilot was, low and behold, none other than Jeffery Carter.

Although there was never enough evidence to arrest Carter as the pilot, law enforcement agencies confirmed that in 1981 he was befriended by infamous pilot and drug smuggler Barry Seal, while Carter was a bartender at a French Quarter bar in New Orleans Louisiana. Seal was from Baton Rouge and was a known smuggler for the Columbian Medellín Cartel.

In 1982, Seal compelled Carter to relocate to Mena, Arkansas, to work for him at Seal's new business called Rich Mountain Aviation at the Mena Airport. It's not certain what Jeffery Carter's responsibilities were, but it's widely believed that Carter was a protégé of Barry Seal and learned flying skills from him.

Dixie Mafia leader Kirksey Nix was suspect in the gangland-style murder of a gambler named Harry Bennett who was about to turn state's evidence against several members. Although Nix's involvement in Bennett's murder was never proven, this incident precipitated a string of killings that left twenty-five people dead in six states over the next four years.

Nix was also suspect in the attempted assassination of McNairy County, Tennessee Sheriff Buford Pusser, and in the murder of Pusser's wife. Nix was convicted of murdering wealthy New Orleans grocery owner Frank Corso. At the time of the murder, Nix was believed to be employed by Darrel Ward in Clarksville, Texas. Ward was a noted associate of Chicago boss Sam "Momo" Giancana and is thought to have controlled much of the organized crime and bootlegging throughout Texas, Louisiana, Arkansas, and Mississippi.

So, who runs the Dixie Mafia today? Depends which state and which prison you are referring to. Kirksey Nix, Jr. is the top dog of the Dixie Mafia. Kirksey, aka "Junior" is serving a life sentence in USP-Terre Haute in Illinois for ordering the murder of Judge Vincent Sherry and the judge's wife, Margaret Sherry in Biloxi, Mississippi. The Sherry murders happened and was ordered by Kirksey Nix while he was serving a life sentence in the Louisiana State Penitentiary at Angola.

Peter "Uncle Pete" Mule is also serving a life sentence in the Louisiana State Penitentiary after being convicted with Kirksey Nix, Jr. for the murder of a New Orleans grocery store owner. "Uncle Pete" is the second highest member of the Dixie Mafia in the United States. It is believed that wealthy business man and known Dixie Mafia member Charles Hilton (Florida panhandle) and pilot and henchman Jeffery Carter (Jasper, Florida) are high level members who are the back bone for Nix today.

State Line Mob

The Dixie Mafia was strongly connected to the State Line Mob and its leader Carl Douglas "Towhead" White. The State Line Mob was an association of criminal elements that operated in the 1950s and 1960s at the Mississippi–Tennessee state line in Alcorn County, Mississippi, and McNairy County, Tennessee, along U.S. Route 45. The State Line Mob was involved in bootlegging, gambling, prostitution, tourist fleecing, robbery, and murder.

The State Line organization owned and operated motels, restaurants, and clubs. These establishments were centers for every form of vice and reaped hundreds of thousands of dollars from sales of illegal moonshine and other contraband products. The primary owners of these businesses were Carl Douglas "Towhead" White, as well as Jack, Louise, and W.O. Hathcock.

A few of the State Line members were originally from Phenix City, Alabama, having been displaced from that town when martial law was declared by the Governor and the Alabama National Guard attempted to clean the town up.

The State Line Mob gained national attention throughout the 1960s for its ongoing feud with famed McNairy County Sheriff Buford Pusser. The film "Walking Tall" and its sequels were based on Pusser's war against the Mob and other criminal elements. Pusser who stood 6'6" died in a car accident on August 24, 1974. He was the feature of a major People Magazine article just a few months earlier.

While these White gangsters were enjoying corruption from local politicians and often protection from local law enforcement, the Black community was being attacked by many of the same forces.

Sources (By Author):

Mr. New Orleans: The Life of a Big Easy Underworld Legend, Brouillette, Frenchy, 2009

The Birth of a Nation, W.D. Griffith, 1915

Mississippi Mud: Southern Justice and the Dixie Mafia, Edward Humes, 1994

The French Quarter: An Informal History of the New Orleans Underworld, Alfred A. Knoff, 1936

What did we learn from Ferguson? Gangsters, Cops, and Politicians Blog, G.Morales, 11/26/14

Chicago Based Gangs: Beyond Folks and People, Joe Sparks, Gabe Morales 2015

Maxine: "Call Me Madam", Maxine Temple Jones, Hardback, 1983

Gangsters Encyclopedia: The World's Most Notorious Mobs, Gangs and Villains, Michael Newton, 2007

How Tall Did Buford Pusser Really Walk?, People Magazine, 4/8/74

Notable Names, The Mob Museum, Las Vegas, NV, 2016

Attorney General's Conference on Organized Crime, 2/15/60, U.S. DOJ

Something wicked this way comes: A historical account of black gangsterism offers wisdom and warning for African-American leadership. Journal of Black Studies, Cureton, S.R., 2009

The Civil Rights Movement Era

As described previously, before the American Civil War almost four million Blacks were enslaved in Southern States. Only White men who owned property could vote and the Naturalization Act of 1790 limited U.S. citizenship to Whites only. Laws enacted in 1790 and 1797 referred to voters as "he or she", and women regularly voted. A law passed in 1807; however, excluded even White women from voting so America was a White male dominated society.

Following the Civil War, three constitutional amendments were passed, including the 13th Amendment (1865) that ended slavery; the 14th Amendment (1868) that gave African Americans citizenship, adding their total population of four million to the official population of southern states for Congressional apportionment; and the 15th Amendment (1870) that gave African-American males the right to vote (only males could vote in the U.S. at the time).

White women could vote again until 1920 when the Nineteenth Amendment was passed that which prohibited state or federal sex-based restrictions on voting. But Black men and women were still prevented from voting via state and local Jim Crow laws enforcing racial segregation in the Southern States.

After returning home from World War II, veteran Medgar Evers decided to vote in a Mississippi election. But when he and some other black ex-servicemen attempted to vote, a White mob stopped them. "All we wanted to be was ordinary citizens," Evers later related. "We fought during the war for America, Mississippi included.

Now, after the Germans and Japanese hadn't killed us, it looked as though the White Mississippians would. . . ."

There were many ways taken to stop Blacks from voting, but one of the most formidable barriers put into place was the literacy test. It required a person seeking to register to vote to read a section of the state constitution and explain it to the county clerk who processed voter registrations. This clerk, who was always White, decided whether a citizen was literate or not. These laws continued in force until 1965 and some say voting discrimination remains in some areas today.

As we said in the Introduction to this book, in order to understand gang problems that came later, one must first understand longstanding political issues that reached every segment of Southern Society. Even though it was an oppressive system, it was a status quo that many southern Whites felt brought stability, law and order.

Once that system came down, there was "White flight" out of many urban areas, increasing migration of southern Blacks to urban areas in the South, up North, and over to the West Coast.

Social tensions, Blacks seeking more voice in local government, and many local Whites fearing changes in their segregationist way of life led to more violence.

The Jim Crow system employed "terror as a means of social control," with the most organized manifestations being the Ku Klux Klan and their collaborators employed in local police departments. This violence played a key role in blocking the progress of the Civil Rights Movement in the late 1950s.

The third and current manifestation of the KKK emerged after 1950, in the form of small, local, unconnected groups that used the KKK name. They focused on opposition to the Civil Rights Movement, often using violence and murder to suppress activists. While these KKK were small in number, they were still feared.

The KKK is considered a Security Threat Group by most correctional systems and by groups like the Southern Poverty Law Center (SPLC) today, but the KKK was basically a gang. Since 1944 there has been no such thing as "the" Ku Klux Klan but instead a variety of different and independent Klan groups, sometimes 50 or more Klan groups at one time, of varying sizes per the Anti-Defamation League.

One individual who was born during this time period is David Duke (1950-present). Duke is a former one-term Republican Louisiana State Representative, he was also a candidate in the Democratic presidential primaries in 1988 and the Republican presidential primaries in 1992. In the late 1960s, Duke met William Luther Pierce, the leader of the White nationalist and anti-Semitic National Alliance, who would remain a lifelong influence on him. Duke joined the Klan in 1967 and graduated from Louisiana State University in 1974. Shortly after graduation, Duke founded the Knights of the Ku Klux Klan (KKKK). He regained fame in the 2016 presidential primary when he backed Republican candidate and presidential elect Donald Trump.

As stated previously by people like Medgar Evers, when African-American soldiers came home from World War II, many felt that they were treated better in other countries than in their own states, especially in the Deep South.

Starting in the early to mid-1950s, churches, local grassroots organizations, fraternal societies, and Black-owned businesses mobilized volunteers to fight for civil rights. They pushed for more rapid change than the traditional approach of mounting court challenges used by the National Association for the Advancement of Colored People (NAACP) formed in 1909 by Moorfield Storey, Mary White Ovington, and renowned Black historian W. E. B. Du Bois.

In 1952, the Regional Council of Negro Leadership (RCNL), led by T. R. M. Howard, a Black surgeon, entrepreneur, and planter, organized a successful boycott of gas stations in Mississippi that refused to provide restrooms for Blacks.

Through efforts of the RCNL, Howard also led campaigns to expose brutality by the Mississippi State Highway Patrol and encouraged Blacks to make deposits in the Black-owned Tri-State Bank of Nashville that gave loans to civil rights activists who were victims of a "credit squeeze" by prejudiced White Citizens' Councils.

The year before, in spring of 1951, several Black students in Virginia protested unequal status in the state's segregated education system. Students at Moton High School protested overcrowded conditions and inadequate educational facilities. Some local NAACP leaders tried to persuade the students to back down from their protest, but the students did not budge. Soon, the NAACP joined their battle and proceeded with multiple court cases challenging school systems; these were later combined under a case known today as Brown v. Board of Education.

On May 17, 1954, the U.S. Supreme Court handed down its decision in Brown v. Board of Education (of Topeka, Kansas). In this case, the plaintiffs, including 3rd grade Topeka student Linda Brown and her father Oliver, charged that the education of Black children in separate public schools from their White counterparts was unconstitutional. The Court stated that the segregation of White and Colored children in public schools had a detrimental effect upon Negroes. The difference impact was deemed greater when it had the sanction of the law with the policy of separating the races usually being interpreted as taking into account the inferiority of Negroes, or Colored people, both common terms at the time.

The day after the Supreme Court's decision, on May 18, 1954, Greensboro, North Carolina, became the first city in the South to publicly announce that it would abide by the ruling. But even in Greensboro, local resistance to desegregation continued, and in 1969, the federal government found the city was not in compliance with the 1964 Civil Rights Act. Transition to a fully integrated school system there did not begin until 1971.

In Southern states such as Alabama, Arkansas, and Virginia, "massive resistance" was practiced by top officials throughout the states. In Virginia, some counties even closed public schools rather than integrate student populations. Many White Christian private schools were founded to accommodate the students who previously went to public schools.

Another racial crisis erupted in Little Rock, AR, on September 4, 1957, when Arkansas Governor Orval Faubus called out the National Guard to stop nine African-American students who sued for the right to attend an integrated Little

Rock Central High School. The nine students were chosen to attend Central High because of their excellent grades. The students had to carpool to school and were escorted by military personnel in jeeps.

The Arkansas Democratic Party, which then controlled politics in the state, put significant pressure on Faubus and he encouraged bringing Arkansas schools into compliance with the Brown decision. Eventually, Faubus then took his stand against it. He was not an avid segregationist and many feel he only fought it to gain political favor with Whites. His resistance received the attention of President Dwight D. Eisenhower, who was determined to enforce orders of the Federal courts. Eisenhower federalized the State National Guard in Arkansas and ordered them to return to their barracks. Eisenhower then deployed elements of the Army's 101st Airborne Division to Little Rock to protect the students. Only one student of the Little Rock Nine, Ernest Green, graduated from Central High School that year. After the 1957–58 school year was over, Little Rock closed its public school system completely rather than continue to integrate after pressure from locals.

Other school systems across the South soon followed suit. It was a mess.

Meanwhile, the Klan and other segregationists were not going down without a fight.

In August, 1955, a fourteen-year-old teen from Chicago, Emmett Till, was visiting relatives in Mississippi when he was kidnapped, brutally beaten, shot, and dumped in the Tallahatchie River allegedly for whistling at a White woman. Two White men, J. W. Milam and Roy Bryant, were arrested for the murder and acquitted by an all-white jury. They later boasted about committing the murder in a Look Magazine interview. The case became a cause célèbre of the Civil Rights Movement and showcased racial injustice in the Deep South.

Local leaders established the Montgomery Improvement Association (MIA) to focus their efforts to highlight extreme forms of segregation. A then little known, Martin Luther King, Jr., was elected President of this organization. The spark that ignited this focus in Montgomery, Alabama, occurred on December 1, 1955, when a Black lady named Rosa Parks refused to give up her seat on a public bus in order to make room for a White passenger. She was arrested, received national publicity, and was hailed as the "Mother of the Civil Rights Movement." Parks was secretary of the Montgomery NAACP chapter and recently returned from a meeting at the Highlander Center in Tennessee where non-violent civil disobedience tactics were taught. African-Americans soon organized a Montgomery Bus Boycott to demand change towards the goal of all passengers being treated equally regardless of race. After the city rejected many of their suggested reforms, the NAACP, led by E.D. Nixon, pushed for full desegregation of public buses.

With the support of most (90%) of Montgomery's 50,000 African Americans, the boycott lasted for 381 days, until the local ordinance segregating Blacks and Whites on public buses was repealed. In November 1956, a federal court ordered Montgomery's buses desegregated and the boycott finally ended.

By 1957, Dr. King and Rev. Ralph Abernathy, leaders of the Montgomery Improvement Association, joined with other church leaders who led similar nationwide boycott efforts, such as Rev. C. K. Steele of Tallahassee, TN, and Rev. T. J. Jemison of Baton Rouge, LA; and other activists such as Rev. Fred Shuttlesworth, Ella Baker, A. Philip Randolph, Bayard Rustin and Stanley Levison, to form the Southern Christian Leadership Conference (SCLC).

The SCLC, with headquarters in Atlanta, Georgia, did not attempt to create a network of national chapters as the NAACP did; rather, it offered training and leadership assistance for local efforts to fight segregation. The organization raised funds, mostly from Northern sources, to support its campaigns. It made non-violence both its central tenet and its primary method of confronting racism. Martin Luther King, Jr. won the 1964 Nobel Peace Prize for his role in the Movement; however, some scholars note that the Movement was far too diverse to just be credited to one person, organization, or strategy.

Out of all the protests, jailing, bloodshed, and sometimes even death during the Movement, came passage of the Civil Rights Act of 1964. This law banned discrimination based on race, color, religion, sex, or national origin in employment practices and ended unequal application of voter registration requirements and racial segregation in schools, at the workplace, and by public accommodations.

The Voting Rights Act of 1965 further restored and protected voting rights. The Immigration and Nationality Services Act of 1965 dramatically opened entry to the U.S. to immigrants other than traditional European groups. While the Fair Housing Act of 1968 banned discrimination in the sale or rental of housing.

 **Alabama Governor George Wallace**

With the implementation of these laws conditions began to get better for most Blacks. But, there was some still resistance and acts of intimidation by Whites in power such as Alabama Governor George Wallace who justified his stance, "A racist is one who despises someone because of his color, and an Alabama segregationist is one who conscientiously believes that it is in the best interest of Negro and White to have a separate education and social order."

This was the theory of "Separate but Equal" quoted by many at the time.

In spite of individuals like Wallace and Klan intimidation, African Americans re-entered politics in the Deep South by the late 1960s. All across the country, young people were inspired to take action. But a wave of inner city riots in black communities from 1964 through 1970 undercut a lot of support from the White community. The emergence of the radical Black Power movement, by individuals like Malcom X, Stokely Carmichael, and organization like the Black Panther Party, lasted from about 1966 to 1975. It challenged the established Black leadership for its cooperative attitude and nonviolence. Instead, it demanded political and economic self-sufficiency by "Any means necessary", even guns.

Freedom Rides were journeys taken by civil rights activists on interstate buses into the segregated Southern States to test the U.S. Supreme Court decision Boynton v. Virginia, (1960), which ruled that segregation was unconstitutional for passengers engaged in interstate travel. The first Freedom Ride of the 1960s left Washington D.C. on May 4, 1961, and was scheduled to arrive in New Orleans on May 17.

In Birmingham, Alabama, an FBI informant reported that Public Safety Commissioner Eugene "Bull" Connor gave Ku Klux Klan members fifteen minutes to attack an incoming group of freedom riders before having police "protect" them. The riders were severely beaten "until it looked like a bulldog had got a hold of them." James Peck, a White activist, was beaten so badly that he required fifty stitches to his head.

When the weary Riders arrived in Jackson, MS, and attempted to use "White only" restrooms and lunch counters they were arrested for Breach of Peace and Refusal to Obey an Officer. Then Mississippi Governor, Ross Barnett, defended the arrests over segregation laws: "The Negro is different because God made him different to punish him." From lockup, the Riders announced they would not pay fines for unconstitutional arrests and illegal convictions and stated by staying in jail they kept the issue in the public eye.

Jailed activists were treated harshly, crammed into tiny, filthy cells and sporadically beaten. In Jackson, some male prisoners were forced to do hard labor in 100+ degree heat. Others were transferred to the Mississippi State Penitentiary at Parchman, where they were treated to harsh conditions. Sometimes the men were tortured by "wrist breakers" suspended from walls. Typically, the windows of their cells were shut tight on hot days, making it very hard for them to breathe.

Public sympathy and support for the Freedom Riders led President John F. Kennedy's administration to order the Interstate Commerce Commission (ICC) to issue a new desegregation order. When the new ICC rule took effect on November 1, 1961, passengers were permitted to sit wherever they chose on the bus; "White" and "Colored" signs came down in the terminals; separate drinking fountains, toilets, and waiting rooms were consolidated; and lunch counters began serving people regardless of skin color.

After the Freedom Rides, local Black leaders in Mississippi such as Medgar Evers asked the SNCC to help register voters and to build community organizations that could win a share of political power in the state. Since Mississippi ratified its new constitution in 1890 with provisions such as poll taxes, residency requirements, and literacy tests, it made registration more complicated and stripped Blacks from voter rolls and voting. In addition, violence at the time of elections had earlier suppressed Black voting.

By the mid-20th century, preventing Blacks from voting had become an essential part of the culture of White supremacy. In the fall of 1961, SNCC organizer Robert Moses began the first voter registration project in McComb and the surrounding counties in the Southwest corner of the state. Their efforts were met with violent repression from state and local lawmen, the White Citizens' Council, and the Ku Klux Klan. Activists were beaten and there were hundreds of arrests of local citizens. Voting activist Herbert Lee was murdered. E.H. Hurst, a member of the Mississippi state legislature, had been threatening to harm activists including Lee. After a coroner's jury ruled the incident justifiable homicide, that Hurst shot in self-defense, there were no further legal proceedings in the Lee murder.

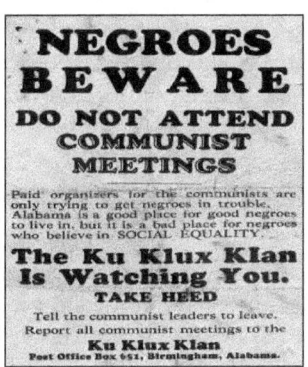

In April 1963, Martin Luther King Jr. was arrested and jailed during anti-segregation protests in Birmingham, AL. He wrote his seminal "Letter from Birmingham Jail," arguing individuals have the moral duty to disobey unjust laws.

Two months later, Medgar Evers, Secretary of the NAACP in Mississippi, was killed. Avowed racist Byran De La Beck, a member of the White Citizens' Council formed in 1954 to resist integration of schools and civil rights activity, was charged Evers' murder twice but released due to hung juries. He was finally convicted 30 years later for the crime and eventually died in prison.

In August, 1963, Martin Luther King Jr. delivered what has been called one of the greatest speeches of all time, his "I Have a Dream" speech to over 200,000 people in Washington D.C. It was a speech that still gives many people chills today.

Eighteen days later, a deadly bombing was deemed an act of White supremacist terrorism which occurred at the African-American 16th Street Baptist Church in Birmingham, Alabama, on Sunday, September 15, 1963. Four members of the Ku Klux Klan planted at least 15 sticks of dynamite attached to a timing device beneath the front steps of the church. Four young Black girls were killed as a result. Radical Professor Angela Davis quotes this event and Birmingham Commissioner of Public Safety Theophilus "Bull" Connor as helping form her views on the U.S. government, of law enforcement, and prison industrial complex.

In 1964, Andrew Young was named executive director of the Southern Christian Leadership Conference (SCLC) and was one of King's key advisors. Young later became a Georgia Congressman, U.S. Ambassador to the United Nations, and Mayor of Atlanta.

There were three separate Selma to Montgomery, Alabama, marches in 1965 to support the Voting Rights Movement. By highlighting racial injustice in the South, they contributed to passage that year of the Voting Rights Act. Activists publicized the three protest marches to walk the 54-mile highway from Selma to the state capital of Montgomery to show the desire of African-American citizens to exercise their constitutional right to vote, in defiance of segregationist repression.

Southern state legislatures had passed and maintained a series of discriminatory requirements and practices that had disenfranchised most of the millions of African Americans across the South since the turn of the century. An African-American group known as The Dallas County Voters League (DCVL) launched a voter's registration campaign in Selma in 1963. Joined by organizers from the Student Nonviolent Coordinating Committee (SNCC), they began working that year in a renewed effort to register Blacks to vote.

In 1963, John Lewis became chairman of the Student Nonviolent Coordinating Committee. He later became director of the Voter Education Project and eventually elected Georgia Congressman in 1986. Lewis was joined by prominent student activists such as Julian Bond who elected to the Georgia House of Representatives in 1965 as part of voting reforms. Stokely Carmichael took over the SNCC in 1966 when Lewis was elected to office. Many activists thought Stokely had ego problems and was not a team player so they nick-named him "Starmichael". He was soon replaced by SNCC leader H. Rap Brown who led a short lived alliance with the Black Panthers. Brown once stated, "If America don't come around, we're gonna burn it down."

Both Lewis and Bond represented the non-violent black ideals of Martin Luther King Jr., while people described Carmichael and H. Rap Brown's philosophies as being more revolutionary and part of the nationalist Black Power Movement.

As Black political efforts grew, the Klan continued its violent war against them.

Sam Bowers, Imperial Wizard of the White Knights of the Ku Klux Klan of Mississippi, sent word in May, 1964 to the Klansmen of Lauderdale and Neshoba Counties that it was time to "activate Plan 4." This plot provided for "the elimination" of despised civil rights activist Michael Schwerner, who the Klan called "Goatee" and "Jew-Boy." Schwerner, the first White civil rights worker based outside of the Mississippi capitol of Jackson, earned the enmity of the Klan by organizing a Black boycott of a White-owned business and aggressively trying to register Blacks to vote in and around Meridian, Mississippi.

On June 21, 1964, Schwerner, and fellow Congress of Racial Equality (CORE) activists Andrew Goodman and James Chaney were stopped by police, allegedly for speeding, then released after dark into the hands of the Ku Klux Klan who murdered them on a lonely road in Neshoba County, Mississippi.

It was an old-fashioned lynching carried out with help of county officials that came to symbolize hardcore Southern resistance. The FBI's search for the conspirators who killed the three young men was depicted in the 1988 movie "Mississippi Burning" starring Gene Hackman and Willem Dafoe as two FBI agents.

The non-violent peaceful protest movement was dealt another blow on February 21, 1965, when Black Muslim radical Malcolm X was gunned down was preparing to address the Organization of Afro-American Unity at the Audubon Ballroom in Manhattan, New York City. This time White racists could not be blamed. He had become a media favorite and some Nation of Islam (NOI) members believed he was a threat to founder Elijah Muhammad's leadership.

Malcolm X, born Malcolm Little, converted to traditional Orthodox Muslim in 1964. He frequently butted heads with Martin Luther King Jr. stating Blacks needed to free themselves of White oppression, "By any means necessary", even if it took violence. His eventual conversion and toning down of race baiting rhetoric might have made King's approach more palatable to some urban Blacks.

On February 26, 1965, activist and Deacon Jimmie Lee Jackson died after being mortally shot several days earlier by a state trooper during a peaceful march in nearby Marion, Alabama. To defuse and refocus the community's outrage, SCLC Director of Direct Action James Bevel, who was directing SCLC's Selma Voting Rights Movement, called for a march of dramatic length, from Selma to the state capital of Montgomery. Bevel had been working on his Alabama Project for voting rights since late 1963.

The first Selma march took place on March 7, 1965, organized locally by Bevel, Amelia Boynton, and others. State troopers and county posse men attacked the unarmed marchers with billy clubs and tear gas after they passed over the county line, and the event became known as "Bloody Sunday". Law enforcement beat Boynton unconscious, and the media publicized worldwide a picture of her lying wounded on the bridge.

The second march took place March 9. Troopers, police, and marchers confronted each other at the county end of the bridge, but when the troopers stepped aside to let them pass, King led the marchers back to the church. He was obeying a federal injunction while seeking protection from federal court for the march. That night, a White group beat and murdered civil rights activist James Reeb, a Unitarian Universalist minister from Boston, who had come to Selma to march with the second group. Many other clergy and sympathizers from across the country also gathered for the second march.

The third march received national and international coverage; it publicized the marchers' message without harassment by police and segregation supporters. Gaining more widespread support from other civil rights organizations in the area, this march was considered an overall success, with greater influence on the public. Voter registration drives were organized in Black-majority areas across the South, but it took time to get people signed up.

While the non-violent Civil Rights Movement by the mid-1960s had achieved many political victories, some blacks felt change was not happening fast enough.

In 1966, the Black Panthers were started by Huey Newton and Bobby Seale in Oakland, CA. The Panthers were often seen open carrying weapons and advocated for violence if necessary. Other chapters soon followed in Los Angeles and Seattle.

Stokely Carmichael, leader of the Student Nonviolent Coordinating Committee (SNCC), coined the phrase "Black Power" in a 1966 speech in Seattle. He defined it as an assertion of Black pride and "the coming together of Black people to fight for their liberation by any means necessary", repeating a line from Malcolm X made in 1965 that said, "So, we only mean vigorous action in self-defense, and that vigorous action we feel we're justified in initiating by any means necessary."

On April 4, 1968, Martin Luther King Jr. was shot dead at the age of 39, as he stood on the balcony outside of the Lorraine Motel in Memphis, Tennessee. Rioting immediately erupted in Chicago, Detroit, Baltimore, Washington D.C. and many other places where Blacks were becoming fed up with the system. Escaped convict and committed racist James Earl Ray was later arrested and convicted of King's assassination.

During his term as U.S. Attorney General Robert F. Kennedy, brother of President John F. Kennedy, became committed to civil rights enforcement. He prosecuted corrupt southern elected officials answered late night calls from Coretta Scott King, wife of Martin Luther Jr., concerning the imprisonment of her husband for demonstrations in Alabama. He demanded that every area of government begin recruiting realistic levels of Black and other ethnic workers, going so far as to criticize Vice President Lyndon B. Johnson for his failure to desegregate his own office staff. Some saw the Kennedy's moves as purely for political gain.

At the time, many southern Democrats where for segregation. Meanwhile, the Republican Party was the "Party of Lincoln". One hundred years later, many Southerners were still not ready to forget Lincoln's attempts at reform.

Prior to the Kennedy Administration, many Blacks voted Republican. The Kennedy's helped secure the release of King from Jail in 1960. After that they were able to convince many Blacks to vote for the Democratic Party.

Robert "Bobby" Kennedy addressed his Presidential Election supporters shortly after midnight on June 5, 1968, in a ballroom at The Ambassador Hotel in Los Angeles, California when he was assassinated by Sirhan, a 24-year-old Palestinian, who opened fire with a .22-caliber revolver. Kennedy was hit three times and five other people also were wounded.

The deaths of Bobby Kennedy and Martin Luther King Jr. in 1968 was the end of an era according to many.

As political discord grew stronger, with leaders overwhelmed or dead, gangs such as the Crips, Bloods, Folks and People, started to step in to address the needs of many young Black males in America.

Sources (By Author):

White Supremacist Prison Gangs in the United States, AntiDefamation League, 2016

Freedom Riders: 1961 and the Struggle for Racial Justice, Raymond Arsenault, 2006

The Autobiography of Martin Luther King, Jr., Clayborne Carson, 2001

Remembering Jim Crow: African Americans Tell About Life in the Segregated South, Edited by William Chafe, Raymond Gavins, and Robert Korstad with Paul Ortiz, Robert Parrish, Jennifer Ritterhouse, Keisha Roberts, and Nicole Waligora-Davis, 2001

Stand up for Alabama: Governor George Wallace, Jeffrey Frederick, 2007

Autobiography of Malcolm, Alex Haley, Attallah Shabazz, 1987

The Selma Voting Rights Struggle & March to Montgomery, Bruce Hartford, 2014

Forgotten: The Untold Story of D-Day's Black Heroes, at Home and at War, Linda Hervieux, 2015

In Peace and Freedom: My Journey in Selma, Bernard LaFayette Jr., 2013

The Life & Times of a Vato Loco, Gabriel C. Morales, 2013

Brown v. Board of Education: A Civil Rights Milestone and Its Troubled Legacy, James T. Patterson, 2001

Rosa Parks: My Story, Rosa Parks, 1991

One Hundred Percent American: The Rebirth and Decline of the Ku Klux Klan in the 1920s, Thomas R. Pegram, 2011

Lessons From Little Rock, Terrance Roberts (Little Rock 9 Student), 2001

Ku Klux Klan, A History of Racism and Violence, Southern Poverty Law Center, 2011

Robert Kennedy: His Life, Evan Thomas, 2000

Black Life in Mississippi, Julius E. Thompson, 2001

Voting Rights Still a Hot-Button Issue, U.S. News 8/4/15

California Style Gangs in the Southeast

According to author and Los Angeles Police Department Detective William "Bill" Dunn, California street gangs have been active since the early 1900s.

While there has been state to state migration, primarily of Mexicans and Mexican-Americans (Chicanos), within the southwest portion of the for about a century due to migration patterns of farmworkers and blue collar workers seeking jobs in large urban cities, there was not a lot of Latino migration into the southeast portion of the U.S. until the 1980s. An exception would be Cubans who fled to Florida during the 1953-58 war against dictator Fulgencio Batista and subsequent refugees who fled after Castro's rise to power and conversion to communism in 1961.

Also of important note, the Mariel Boatlift which was a mass emigration of Cubans who departed from Cuba's Mariel Harbor for the United States between April 15 and October 31, 1980. People involved in this boatlift were often called "Marielitos".

This just so happened to precede the "Crack Cocaine Epidemic" and fueled the growth of the Cocaine Cowboys, Columbian Drug Cartels, and their Cuban counterparts.

Of course, most of the migrants and immigrants coming into the country were law abiding for the most part, even if they were undocumented workers.

But, this started to change in the 1980s in the southeast United States.

In L.A., while Crips and Bloods became more famous in the 1980s for crack cocaine sales, Chicano street gangs were also involved.

Late 1800s-Early 1900s

During the 1890s, the population of African Americans in Los Angeles increased from 1,258 to 2,131. By 1920, African American's in the city numbered over 15,000. This continued at a trickle, then grew tremendously during the World War II Era to 63,774 by 1940 as Blacks sought better jobs and pay. This growing mass migration on the West Coast was similar to the impact of post-Civil War wave of Blacks moving north into urban cities like Chicago.

1940s

Gang researcher (Alex) Alonso identified the formation of African-American gangs in Los Angeles in the late 1940s. Alonso proposed it was "racial intimidation, school and residential segregation, extreme marginalization and racial exclusion," not "economic restructuring, deindustrialization, population shifts, and poverty" that played significant roles in the formation of African-American gangs in Los Angeles.

During the 1940s, resentment of Blacks by Whites grew in Los Angeles as many African Americans challenged the legal housing discrimination laws. Those laws prevented them from purchasing property outside the original settlement neighborhoods, and kept them from integrating the public schools. In the late 1940s, the first major Black clubs appeared in Los Angeles.

In the musical biography based film "Ray", starring Jamie Fox, there is a scene where he goes from Seattle down to a majority Black patron club in L.A. with Blues player Lowell Fulson. The nightclub scene in Los Angles became greater with the growing Black population, this often included Black gang members.

As a result of more Blacks, frequently from places like Louisiana and Mississippi, moving into communities like South Central Los Angeles, Watts, and Compton, many Whites began to move out. This is often referred to as "White flight".

Most Blacks were simply looking for a better life that they had in the South. Moving out West offered more employment opportunities in factories and an escape from Southern oppression. These moves turned out to be the trigger for traditional White supremacist ideology, institutional inequality (in housing, education, and employment), and restrictions relative to where Blacks could socialize. That led to a regional civil rights movement between 1946 and 1950."

Blacks were referred to housing in growing Black areas under racist housing covenants in a system often referred to as "red lining". This came from mortgage loaner and landlords drawing red lines on maps "where Blacks should live".

From 1945-1948, many Black residents challenged restrictive housing covenants in court. These attempts prompted the resurfacing of the Ku Klux Klan in L.A. and some White youths formed street clubs to battle integration in both the community and schools of Black residents.

One of the most infamous groups of White youth were the Spook Hunters. The name of this club emphasized their racist attitude towards Blacks, "Spook" being a derogatory term for them. The club members' jackets had an animated Black face with exaggerated facial features with a noose hanging around the neck. If Blacks were seen outside of "their area", they were often attacked.

1950-60s

Prior to the late 1960s, Black gang activity was mostly limited to conflicts with other racial groups, as well as drinking alcohol, gambling, and committing misdemeanor crimes. Gangs were typically turf-oriented and seldom left their neighborhoods. By the 1960s, some politicians tried to harness the power and unity of the gangs for their own political benefit by encouraging gang members to participate in political rallies, demonstrations, and public discussions. The Black population in Los Angeles leapt from approximately just under 64,000 in 1940 to about 350,000 in 1965, rising from 4% of LA's population to 14% of the total.

Mid 1960s-70s

The Watts Riots took place from August 11-16, 1965. On August 11, 1965, an African American motorist was arrested for drunk driving. A minor roadside argument broke out and then escalated into a fight with police. The community reacted in outrage to allegations of police brutality that soon spread. Six days of looting and arson followed. Los Angeles police needed the support of nearly 4,000 members of the California Army National Guard to help quell the riots. The Los Angeles Police Department (LAPD) put down the riot by force; thus, there were even more cries of police brutality. It resulted in 34 deaths and over $40 million in property damage. It was the city's worst unrest until the Rodney King riots of 1992.

Blacks responded with a more powerful version of community self-defense, the

Black Panther Party for Self Defense. Black urban youth were attracted to the Panthers' defiant speech, bold display of guns, and military styled organization. The Panthers' appeal spread in great part because it directly recruited frustrated, angry youth who felt alienated from mainstream society and older males who were already involved in gangs. More chapters were soon started across the country." As a result of the FBI's counterintelligence program (COINTELPRO), many Black Panther leaders were arrested and imprisoned, some were killed.

Former Black Liberation Army member Clark Squire, aka Sundiata Alcoli, who was sentenced in 1974 for murdering a New Jersey State trooper, claims that Alprentice "Bunchy" Carter and Raymond Washington, both leaders of street organizations were very much attracted to the Black Panthers. Carter was a gang member in the Slauson Renegades, an organization that predated both the Crips and Bloods by many years. The Slausons started in 1952 and were defunct by 1965 according to Alex Alonso. Carter was killed in 1969 and there is no hard law enforcement documentation or anywhere else that he was ever a Crip member. Washington, the sole founder, organized the Crips in 1969 at the age of fifteen and was much younger than Carter who was 36 years old when he died.

Washington was from the Eastside of South Central L.A. and originally ran with a gang called the Baby Avenues. His gang renamed themselves the Eastside Crips and soon joined forced with Westside Crips led by Stanley "Tookie" Williams who had been kicked out of the Gladiators street gang and "Big Jamel" Barnes from the Avalon Gardens Crips. The Eastside and Westside Crips were soon joined by gangsters who became Compton Crips.

According to Acoli, Crips members were originally identified as "Community Relations for an Independent People" or "Community Revolution In Progress" (CRIP), a community helping association. With changes in leadership, following and resources, the Crips shifted to more self-centered activities such as drug distribution and weapon trafficking. Many gang researchers and practitioners disagree with the claims that the CRIPS were started as a benevolence organization. This is backed up by retired cops, including Zach Fortier, a police officer for over 30 years who interviewed Raymond Washington's nephew about roots of gang in his biography "I am Raymond Washington".

Gabriel Morales also strongly feels this version is not a historical fact, but may be BGF influence, a prison gang few Crips ever join. Another myth is that the Crips branched off from the Black Panthers and imitated them for their black leather jackets. This is not true either Black leather jackets were one of the most prized possessions for many Black youth all across America, not just in L.A. The Crips were common thugs and could care less about helping the community. They mostly preyed on other Blacks, something the Panthers were strongly against. What it is true that the Crips and other Black gangs filled the void for disillusioned Black youth after many of the Panthers were killed or locked up in the early 1970s.

Morales feels there are many different versions of how the name "Crips" came to be about and none of them are documented for 100% sure. Some people will state that founder Washington carried around a picture of a "baby crib", but decided to call the gang "Crips", how silly does that sound? Some will say it came from the comic book "Tales from the Crypt", but there is little evidence of this either.

The most likely reason for the gang's name was the way they walked which was a ditty-bop strut as if crippled. Today, there is even a dance called "Crip Walk" during which the letters C-R-I-P are spelled out with the feet.

Some Bloods today also claim that they can trace the lineage of their organization in the Black Panther Party. Acoli suggested that the leaders of the gangs that became the Bloods formed a constitution that was patterned on the constitution of the Black Guerilla Family (BGF), the organization that many Black Panthers started when they were incarcerated at San Quentin State Prison.

Morales, who also wrote a book on the BGF, feels that Acoli and others are confusing early 1980s prison gangs, the United Blood Nation and United Blood Line that were influenced by BGF but started in prison well after the Bloods and Pirus were established on the street in the early 1970s.

The first Blood sets actually came out of Compton on Piru Street and was started by Vincent "Pudding" Scott and Sylvester Owens. As the Crips began to rapidly spread throughout the Greater Los Angeles area, often converting existing local gangs to add Crip to their name, non-Crip gang sets like the Pirus became known as Bloods or "anti-Crip". Soon, the polarization among L.A. Black youth gangs became so strong that they were given an option, "become Crip or die!" Those who refused, Compton Pirus, and gangs outside of Compton like Brims, Bishops, and Bounty Hunters, joined under the banner of "Bloods".

Black Lives Matter

These same ideologies of people like Sundiata Alcoli or Yusef Jah and Sister Shah'keyah who wrote "Uprising" a mythological account of the 1992 Rodney

King Riots and how Crips and Bloods became political activists have evolved to the present date with the "Black Lives Matter" (BLM) movement that had its start in the southeast portion of the U.S. where police community relations can be poor.

BLM was started after the 2013 acquittal of racist vigilante George Zimmerman in the 2012 shooting death of African-American teen Trayvon Martin in Florida. BLM soon became nationally recognized for its street demonstrations following the 2014 deaths of two African Americans. One was Michael Brown, resulting in protests and rioting against police in Ferguson, Missouri. In their efforts to expose police brutality, BLM was a major force in the protest slogan, "Hands up, don't shoot!" This was proved later to be a false narrative of what occurred, but BLM continued to use it. The death of Eric Garner at the hands of police using a use force caught on video that was questionable for a man only standing on the street selling single cigarettes resulted in unrest in New York City.

These two incidents, and others, were fueled in part by the New Black Panther Party (NBPP) and BGF operatives in the community. The NBPP is a U.S.-based Black political organization founded in Dallas, Texas, in 1989 that is not directly tied to the original Panthers. The Black Guerrilla Family (BGF) has its roots in the California system and dates back to the mid-1960s under radical prisoner George Jackson. BGF leaders also communicated with BLM leaders.

Their official website states: Black Lives Matter is an ideological and political intervention in a world where Black lives are systematically and intentionally targeted for demise. It is an affirmation of Black folks' contributions to this society, our humanity, and our resilience in the face of deadly oppression

The BLM website also alleges Blacks are systematically and intentionally targeted for demise in some kind of nationwide conspiracy. Many law enforcement officers feel extremist elements of BLM has less to do with saving "Black Lives", even Black Officers' lives, but instead is focused as anti-law enforcement/anti-establishment with covert ideologies of violent revolutionary movements. This is shown when dozens of marchers in downtown New York City were egged on by a radical agitator shouting, "What do we want?", the reply by about 100 BLM marchers was "Dead Cops!" The agitator continued, "When do we want it?", the protestors yelled back, "Now!" BLM propaganda is seen in T-shirts and posters of "The Pigs" killing Blacks or Isis-like black clad figures cutting cops' throats.

It should be noted that BLM is a very diverse group and not all supporters hate cops. Many who sympathize with BLM just want to see more reform in the system.

California Gang Migration to the Southeastern U.S.

The American crack epidemic was a surge of crack cocaine use in major cities across the United States between 1984 and the early 1990s.

At the same time this scourge was affecting American cities, Crips and Bloods from the Greater Los Angeles area found they could make a much larger profit selling it in other cities and states. As a result, Crips and Bloods spread north and eastward like wildfire. For instance, Bloods are currently the biggest gang problem in South Carolina today.

Gang War: Bangin' in Little Rock, often referred to as Gang Bangin' in Little Rock, is a 1994 HBO documentary about street gangs in Little Rock, Arkansas.

The documentary brought much attention to the crime problems in the capitol city that is approximately 50% White and 50% non-White. Following TV airing of the show, the Little Rock Police force was quadrupled. As a result, the street gang problem was nearly eradicated for a while. Steve Nawojczyk was the County Coroner during the Gang War years and featured in the documentary. He continues to work in the intervention and prevention of youth gangs today. While Gang War: Bangin' in Little Rock followed Nawojczyk while he did his grim work of identifying dead bodies, it also showed his attempts at reducing the record-high homicide rate by talking to young people.

In 2012, the National Gang Center reported the existence of approximately 30,700 gangs (an increase from 29,900 in 2011) and 850,000 gang members (an increase from 782,500 in 2011) throughout 3,100 jurisdictions with gang problems (down from 3,300 in 2011).

At the same time, the National Gang Intelligence Center reported 9,871 gangs with more than 172,360 members in the Southeast Region. The most significant gangs were the Crips and Sureños 13 who mainly originated in Los Angles, Gangster Disciples and Latin Kings who originated in Chicago, and an East Coast version of the United Blood Nation (UBN).

 **Gang Graffiti in Memphis, TN**

By the year 2000, Memphis PD reported Florencia 13, Tristes, Pelones, Krazy Ass Latinos, and Sureños 13, being active in a city that known more for Black gangs.

The National Gang Intelligence Center also noted the following trends:

• The presence of MS 13 in North Carolina and Georgia is growing. For instance, in October, 2016, two MS-13 gang members were sentenced to life in prison on Tuesday for their roles in separate murders. The two were among 37 MS-13 gang members named in a federal indictment involving racketeering conspiracy

• The increased migration of Hispanic gangs into the region has resulted in violent confrontations with local African American gangs for control of gang territories.

• Mexican DTOs have increased their criminal operations in the region over the past few years, providing gangs, particularly Hispanic gangs, in the region with a steady supply of drugs that they have used to expand their drug distribution operations.

Sureños and MS13 in North Carolina

The NGIC predicted that:

• Hispanic gangs will expand drug distribution operations in the Southeast Region.

• Hispanic gangs will establish more direct associations with Mexican sources of supply for drugs.

• Hispanic gangs will take a more active role in developing independent transportation and distribution networks in the region.

• Some Hispanic gangs in the Southeast Region will transition from retail-level drug sales to wholesale-level distribution, which may lead to violent confrontations with other wholesale drug distributors in the region.

Sureños 13 Graffiti in Alabama, South Carolina, and Tennessee

Latino gangs in Alabama come from all over. In past years, the biggest threat were gangs that migrated from Atlanta, specifically Malditos 13, which was connected to Georgia's La Gran Familia conglomerate. That threat has now waned.

The most serious gang in Central Alabama, is La Quemada (LQ) meaning "The Burned". LQ was imported from Inglewood, CA, as a spinoff group of Inglewood 13. They maintained their Inglewood heritage as was observed in their graffiti and social site postings. Drug trafficking/warehousing/money protection/new and high quality firearms/prostitution/gang-on-gang assaults, and possible murders, although not fully documented/cartel connections.

Their current numbers are documented at around 20, but a LQ sub-clique, called the "Youngsters" boasted nearly 100 around the year 2010. Like in much of the rest of America, it is believed that the Mexican Drug Cartels have quieted the street gangs so as not to draw attention to their operations.

Sources (By Author):

An updated history of the new Afrikan prison struggle. Acoli, S., James, J., 2003

Gang Report, Birmingham PD, 2015

2 MS-13 gang members sentenced to life, Charlotte Observer, 11/1/16

The Gangs of Los Angeles, William Dunn, 2007

Gang Report, Fairfax PD, 2015

The Mariel Exodus Twenty Years Later, Gastón Fernández, 2002

I am Raymond Washington, Zach Fortier, 2015

Ray, Taylor Hacket, Universal Pictures, 2004

Gang War: Bangin' in Little Rock, HBO Entertainment, 1994

Latino Gangs Training, ILGIA-Tuscaloosa, AL, 2010

Race & Place in the Adaptation of Mariel Exiles", International Migration Review, 2001

Uprising, Yusef Jah, Sister Shah'keya, 1997

Chicano Gangs and History of the Southwest U.S., S.Lucero, G.Morales, 2014

Gang Report, Memphis PD, 2000

The History of the Black Guerilla Family, Gabe Morales, 2013, Rev. 2016

Varrio Warfare: Violence in the Latino Community. Gabriel C. Morales, 1998

Gang Report, National Gang Center, 2012

Gang Report, National Gang Intelligence Center, 2012

Globalization to a Latin Beat: The Miami Growth Machine, Annals of the American Academy of Political and Social Science, Jan Nijman, 1997

Gang Report, South Carolina-DOC, 2016

Officers prepare for gangs to emerge, Tuscaloosa News, 4/16/10

The Projects: Gang and Non-Gang Families in East Los Angeles, James Vigil, 2008

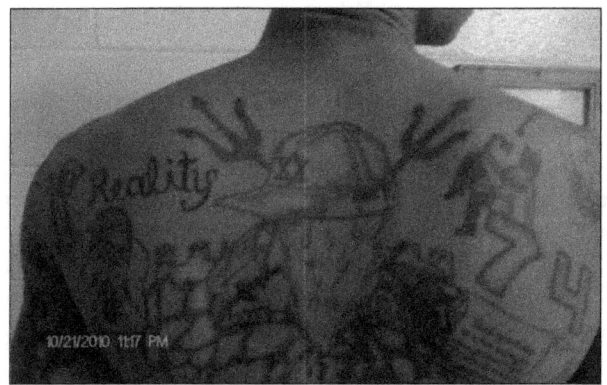

Chicago Style Gangs in the Southeast

Evidence of Black street gangs in Chicago did not appear until the 1920s. Perkins asserted that "Blacks who in lived in Chicago before 1930 were mostly second-generation Southerners." The residences of those Blacks were typically confined to underdeveloped, segregated areas. That compounded the overcrowding problem in the substandard housing that was available. Many of the males were chronically unemployed resulting in many spending countless idle hours out in the street.

In 1927, Frederic M. Thrasher wrote one of the first major gang studies and identified the 1,313 early gangs (with an estimated 25,000 members) active in Chicago's neighborhoods including groups with names such as the Onions, Kenwoods, hard-boiled Crawfords, and Bloody Broomsticks. Thrasher reported that most of the Chicago gang activity in the 1860s consisted of breaking fences and stealing cabbages from people's gardens, as there was "not much else to take". Gang activity in the 1880s included the Hickory Street gang, who spent their time reading, as well as "play(ing) cards, study(ing), and drink(ing) their beer".

Renowned author and gang researcher Joan Moore found that the dominance of Chicago's White ethnic gangs ended shortly after Thrasher's research was completed. Thrasher found that "the gangs of the 1920s were largely a one-generation immigrant ghetto phenomenon."

Between 1910 and 1930, during the Great Migration of more than a million Blacks from the southern states, Chicago gained almost 200,000 Black residents giving the city an enormous urban Black population along with New York City, Cleveland, Detroit, Philadelphia, and other Northeast and Midwest cities.

In Thrasher's study of Chicago gangs, he observed a gang in Chicago during the 1920s called the Dirty Dozens who often attacked Black youths with knives, blackjacks, and revolvers because of racial differences. Black gangs in Chicago likely formed to protect their members (and perhaps their neighborhood) from gangs of White youth. During the Chicago race riots of 1919, the Dirty Dozen gang had several members, according to Thrasher, who chased and threatened several Black men in the Black Belt (a 30-block stretch of run-down housing on the South side), as members of the gang had assumed a mob mentality.

Black history expert Steven R. Cureton traced the origin of Chicago's serious Black street gangs to the segregated inner-city areas, beginning in the early 1900s. Cureton argued that the street gang (not the family or the church) was the most important social network organization for urban youth, even though it was the surest way to end up a felon, convict, or dead.

The proliferation of gangs in most major urban areas, and even in some smaller poverty-stricken areas, was significantly related to Black migration and overcrowding in socially disorganized areas. There often was a subculture of conflict deviance, crime, and violence, dysfunctional family dynamics, and blocked access to legitimate opportunities, among other factors.

Cureton summarized that the origins of contemporary street gangs was traced to Blacks' disproportionate residency in socially disorganized inner-city areas between 1917 and the early 1920s. The relatively swift conversion in Chicago from traditionally White neighborhoods to Black yielded tremendous interracial conflict between White youth and the street-corner congregations of Black males. White youth were interested in the right to remain racially segregated, and Black youth were interested in achieving more social freedoms.

1930s to mid-1960s

Challenges from White and other non-Black immigrant groups declined in the later years of the 1920s and the early 1940s, giving rise to interracial conflict and competition for the ghetto's scarce resources and control of the underground drug market.

By the start of the 1930s, gangs had been established in most of Chicago's African American communities. The public school system was "ineffective and alienating" for Blacks, and unemployment in the 1930s was said to be eroding traditional family structures. Active racial discrimination limited the number of legitimate employment opportunities, while the number of illegal employment opportunities flourished, tied to the notorious political machine that was active in Chicago.

In Joe Sparks and Gabe Morales' book, Chicago Based Gangs: Beyond Folks & People, they note that future Mayor of Chicago, Richard J. Daley, was President of the Hambergs, a known White political intimidation group (gang). Another White gang active at the time were the Ragens, sponsored by Cook County Commissioner Frank Ragen. Other gangs operated in similar fashion intimidating local Blacks.

Later Years 1966-Present

Modern Chicago street gangs can be traced to the 1960's when the Blackstone Rangers developed from a loosely organized youth group into a criminal organization. The group's leader, Jeff Fort, allied the gang with many other area street gangs to form a new organization, calling it the Black P-Stone Nation.

Contemporary gangs in Chicago typically follow one of two alliances: Folk or People. These alliances were established in the Illinois prison system for protection. As the Florida Department of Corrections explains, People Nation and Folk Nation are not gangs, they are alliances. A comparison, according to the FDOC website, is the National and American baseball leagues. The National League is not a team, it is the alliance in which teams like the L.A. Dodgers and Atlanta Braves play baseball. The American League is the alliance in which the Baltimore Orioles and New York Yankees play ball.

The Folk Nation includes Gangster Disciples, La Raza, Latin Disciples, Simon City Royals, Spanish Cobras, Supreme Gangsters, and several other smaller gangs.

The People Nation includes Latin Kings, Vice Lords, 4 Corner Hustlers, Black P Stones, Cobra Stones, El Rukns, Latin Counts, and a few smaller gangs.

In the early 1990s, four major gangs were said to have a foundation in the Chicago, IL area by the Federal Bureau of Investigation (FBI):

- Gangster Disciples
- Vice Lords

- Latin Kings
- Latin Disciples

There are many Chicago based gangs active in the Southeast United States.

Gangster Disciples

 **A very young Larry Hoover**

The Gangsters Disciples have roots that date back to the 1960s. They are part of the Folks Nation, and fall under the 6 point star. Future GD leader Larry Hoover was born on November 30, 1950 in Jackson, Mississippi. In 1955, his family moved to Chicago. In 1964, Hoover joined the Supreme Gangsters, becoming the leader of the gang the following year. They later were referred to as Gangster Disciples. Meanwhile, a slightly older David Barksdale was born in Sallis, Mississippi. He moved to Chicago with his parents in 1957. Barksdale also became involved in the gang lifestyle in Chicago and in 1966 Barksdale's gang absorbed several other gangs and became known as the Black Disciples. In 1969, Barksdale propositioned Hoover to merge the two organizations as the Black Gangster Disciple Nation. Barksdale proposed that they share equal power and Hoover agreed. When Barksdale died in 1974, the umbrella organization remained as the Black Gangster Disciples. In 1978, the Black Gangsters, Gangster Disciples, and Black Disciples split away from the Black Gangster Disciples unification. Hoover is and has been the leader of the Gangster Disciples since 1974. The group is structured like a corporation and is led by a "Chairman of the Board". The Gangster Disciples often align themselves with Crips in some areas of the U.S.

A group identifying themselves as the Insane Gangsta Disciples of Tuscaloosa, Alabama, posted their philosophy on Facebook: *"what the Folk Nation is all about . . . commonly confused as a street gang . . . Gangs are all about making themselves rich and usually at the expense of their community, gangs are nothing but united street thugs that commit criminal activities. Folk Nation members are different, our purpose is to build our community, protection of our community members, making sure that our youth is educated, and to guide the newer generation into getting political jobs.*"

 **GDs in Mobile, Alabama**

In Georgia, incarcerated members of the Gangster Disciples coerce other young men to join. Shortly after he turned 18, Cortez Berry was assaulted and publicly humiliated by gang members claiming membership in the gang. Berry reported that fellow inmates at the Al Burruss Correctional Training Center in Forsyth, GA tried to get him to join the Gangster Disciples. When he refused, the men beat him severely and posted embarrassing pictures of him on Facebook with the caption *"WEN YHU DISRESPECT DA NATION...IT BRINGZ NUTHIN BUT PAIN & SUFFERINGG.."* The pictures showed Berry crouched below two other men standing over him with his eye swollen shut and a leash around his neck.

The Gangster Disciples and their Folk Nation allies, 74 Hoover Crips, even threatened law enforcement in Jackson, Mississippi. Apparently some of the older gang members were trying to stop it, but the younger gang members were trying to make a name for themselves. The Folk Nation, namely Gangster Disciples, is the most predominant gang in the State of Mississippi. The most prevalent gangs in southern Mississippi are Simon City Royals, Gangster Disciples, Latin Kings, Crips, Bloods, and Vice Lords. The Gangster Disciples are involved in the illegal drug trade. The Simon City Royals are known for committing burglaries, robberies, and selling prescription medication. The Gangster Disciples, representing the organization as "Brothers of the Struggle," recently organized the

"13th annual Brothers of the Struggle Weekend." Events in Hattiesburg, MS, included a concert, a party, and an after-party event.

Gangster Disciples in Chicago have received guns via the "iron pipeline" that feeds guns to Illinois from states like Mississippi through straw purchasers. Besides the Cook County suburbs, those states are the biggest suppliers of crime guns to Chicago. Some gun traffickers have familial ties. Like Hoover and Barksdale's families, they went up to Chicago for work and left behind family in Mississippi. Firearms also are cheaper in Mississippi, and firearms laws in Mississippi are a lot more lax than in Illinois. In Mississippi, gun owners are not required to go through a state background check to obtain a permit. They only have to present a valid driver's license or state ID to a gun store and then pass a background check.

Gangster Disciples also sell drugs and commit violent crimes in Memphis, TN. Members are known to have transported drugs to Memphis using Greyhound buses and the U.S. Postal Service. The GDs have long been considered the most visible and violent street gang in Memphis, TN, and have been active there since the mid-1980s. Elsewhere in the state, a Chattanooga area judge rebuked a Gangster Disciple as he appeared in court, "Sir, East Lake Courts is not your hood, it's the citizens of the United States who own that because they work and pay taxes. You don't own that . . . People like you have made it a violent, unsafe place to live and hopefully we can make it the place that it used to be." GDs have a rapidly growing presence in Middle Tennessee, too. The local Gangster Disciples' motto is "more money and more power." In recent years, the gang has increased their presence in larger cities like Nashville, Clarksville, and Murfreesboro. The ATF has matched the Gangster Disciples to dozens of local shootings and drug deals.

 **BPS Leader Jeff Fort as a young man**

Black P-Stones (BPS) founder Jeff Fort was from Aberdeen, Mississippi, and moved as a young boy with his family to Chicago, but frequently went back to the

South. The BPS are part of the People Nation. In 1987, Fort was tried and convicted for conspiring with Libya to perform acts of domestic terrorism. He is currently housed at the ADX-Supermax prison in Florence, Colorado.

Vice Lords

The Vice Lords are the oldest street gang in Chicago, are part of the People Nation, thus fall under the 5 point star. The gang was called the Conservative Vice Lord Nation, was founded by a group of unidentified juveniles in 1958 at the Illinois State Training School for boys. The Vice Lord Nation is led by a national board and most of its members are African American males. The Vice Lords were one of two major street gangs in Memphis, TN. The gang has been entrenched in Memphis neighborhoods and active there since the mid-1980s.

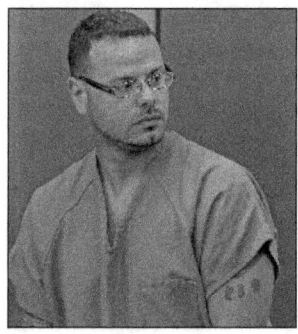
Former Florida Inca Luis Toledo

Latin Kings

The Latin Kings (aka, Latin King and Queen Nation), Almighty Latin Charter Nation (ALCN), Almighty Latin King and Queen Nation (ALKQN) is the largest

Latino gang east of the Mississippi. According to the National Gang Crime Research Center (NGCRC), the actual genesis of the Latin Kings was about 1964-65. Others claim it dates back to the 1940s. The Latin Kings are highly organized, with leadership at the national, regional, and local levels with ranks such as "Inca". The organization is governed by a Constitution with established rules and by-laws. The gang consists predominately of Latino members. Some chapters also have female associates, commonly referred to as Latin Queens. The Latin Kings can be found primarily in Chicago/Mid-West, New York/New Jersey, Texas, and Florida. According to Gabe Morales, Joe Sparks who worked Chicago PD Gang Unit, Edwin Santana who worked a New Jersey Gang Unit, and Lou Savelli who worked NYPD Gang Unit, there are actually several different versions of the Latin Kings.

The first is the Chicago original, also called "King Motherland-Chicago" (KMC). The Chicago version is the largest and has a stable infrastructure ensuring loyalty of members by fear and discipline. During the 1980s, within the confines of the Connecticut prison system, inmates Nelson L. Millet and Pedro Millan reassessed the direction of the Latin Kings and on writing the new charter created the Almighty Latin Charter Nation (ALCN). In 1986, Luis "King Blood" Felipe, expanded the ideologies of Chicago and Connecticut to formed the New York State "Almighty Latin King & Queen Nation" (ALKQN) within the confines of the Collins Correctional Facility in New York. In 1996, under the blessing of "King Blood", the ALKQN appointed Antonio "King Tone" Fernandez as the new leader of the ALKQN New York State Bloodline.

Like Felipe, Fernandez was eventually housed in the Federal Bureau of Prisons. He was incarcerated at one time in USP-Pollock in Louisiana where he was disciplined in 2004 for violating regulations. Strict laws within the Nation read, "No member shall conduct an interview with any person from the news media concerning Nation's affairs without the approval of Las Coronas".

Since 2007, a mission to unite the group, the Chicago and New York leadership under the KMC has led to a universal "Almighty Latin King & Queen Nation" title change on much of the East Coast. The Latin Kings began spreading into Florida in the mid-1990s. Most Latin Kings in Florida were Bloodline off-shoots and did not report to Chicago. As a result, their structure is not as disciplined. They are being closely monitored to see if they will fall in line with King Motherland Chicago.

Maniac Latin Disciples

The Latin Disciples, also known as Maniac Latin Disciples originated in Chicago in the mid-1960s. Most members are Latinos. The Maniac Latin Disciples is the largest Hispanic gang in the Folk Nation Alliance. The gang is most active in the Great Lakes Region and can sometimes be found in states like Florida. While there are not a huge number of Maniac Latin Disciples in the Southeast, one of the most famous was Jose Padilla, also known as the "Dirty Bomber", who was radicalized in a Florida corrections facility.

International Posse and Imperial Gangsters

The InterNational Posse (INP) multi-ethnic gang originated in South Dade County, Florida, as protection against Latin Kings. They soon joined the Folk Nation.

Imperial Gangsters (IGN) also have a significant presence in the Miami area. IG members often use a pink panther with a crown symbol, they fall under Folk Nation. In 2014, ten alleged members of the Almighty Imperial Gangsters Nation were indicted by a federal grand jury in the Southern District of Florida for their roles in various murders in Miami, Chicago, and East Chicago.

Sources:

Gangster Disciples, ChicagoGangs.org, 2016

Something wicked this way comes: A historical account of Black gangsterism offers wisdom and warning for African-American leadership. Journal of Black Studies, Cureton, S.R., 2009

Black Gangster Disciples; Racketeering Enterprise Investigations, FBI-Memphis Division, 1993

Gang Profile - Vice Lord Nation. FBI-Organizational Intelligence Unit, 1994

Gang and Security Threat Group Awareness, Florida DOC Website, 2016

Latino Gangs, University of Illinois-Chicago, GangResearch.Net, 2003

Attorney General's Report to Congress on the Growth of Violent Street Gangs in Suburban Areas. Appendix B. National-Level Street, Prison, and Outlaw Motorcycle Gang Profiles: STREET GANGS, National Drug Intelligence Center, 2008

Gang Threat Analysis: The Black Disciples. National Gang Crime Research Center, George W. Knox, 2004

National Gang Threat Assessment, National Gang Intelligence Center, 2009

Knox, G.C. (2010). Gang Profile: The Latin Kings. National Gang Crime Research Center.

Latin Kings, North Carolina Gang Investigators Association, 2015

Insane Gangsta Disciples, Facebook page of Insane Gangsta Disciples, 2014

Latin Kings hit Florida in 1990s, state's largest gang, Orlando Sentinel, 11/28/14

Georgia Inmate Beating Was on Facebook Before Guards Knew, NBC News, 4/3/15

Police vigilant as 'credible' gang threats surface, The Clarion-Ledger, 5/19/15

Gang violence more prevalent in South MS than most realize. WLOX-TV, 5/13/15

Alleged gang convention in Hattiesburg causes concern among officials, The Clarion-Ledger, 6/2/15

Straw purchasers help convicts get around the law and get armed. Chicago Sun-Times, Frank Main, 8/28/12

East Coast Gangs: Then and Now, Savelli, Santana & Morales, 2016

Chicago Based Gangs: Beyond Folks & People, Joe Sparks, Gabe Morales, 2015

The Gangs: A study of 1,313 gangs in Chicago, New Chicago School Press, Thrasher, F.M., 1927, Reprinted 2000

Simon City Royals gang members arrested, WLOX, 11/23/16

22 people indicted after OCU undercover investigation, WMCA-TV, 4/17/15

Judge to gang member: "East Lake Courts is not your hood" WRCB-TV, 4/16/15.

Gangster Disciples growing rapidly in middle Tennessee. WSMV-TV, 4/13/15

Down-South Homegrown Gangsters

The 2005 Hurricane Katrina was the costliest natural disaster, as well as one of the five deadliest hurricanes, in the entire history of the United States. The storm is currently ranked as the third most intense United States landfall tropical cyclone, behind only the 1935 Labor Day hurricane and Hurricane Camille in 1969. Overall, at least 1,245 people died in the hurricane and subsequent floods, making it the deadliest United States natural disaster since the 1928 Okeechobee hurricane. Total property damage was estimated at $108 billion (2005 USD), roughly four times the damage wrought by Hurricane Andrew in 1992.

Hurricane Katrina effected thousands of people including the criminal element.

Some residents of New Orleans who remained in the city began looting stores. Many were in search of food and water that were not available to them through any other means, as well as non-essential items. Additionally, there were reports of carjacking, murders, thefts, and rapes in New Orleans. Some sources later determined many of the reports were inaccurate, greatly exaggerated or completely false, leading news agencies to print retractions.

Thousands of National Guard troops were mobilized and sent to Louisiana, with 7,841 in the area on August 29, to a maximum of 46,838 on September 10, 2005. A number of local law enforcement agents from across the country were also temporarily deputized by the state as residents feared anarchy on the streets. "They have M16s and are locked and loaded. These troops know how to shoot and kill and I expect they will," Louisiana Governor Kathleen Blanco said.

Several shootings occurred between police and New Orleans residents, some involving police misconduct; including an incident that killed two unarmed civilians and seriously injured other others later deemed innocent at Danziger Bridge. Five former police officers pleaded guilty to charges connected to the bridge shootings. Overall, a number of arrests were made throughout the affected area, including some near the New Orleans Convention Center. A temporary jail was constructed of chain link cages in the New Orleans Union Passenger Terminal, the city's main train station.

In addition, numerous stories were reported that, in the absence of law and order, White vigilantes decided who should live and who should die. Shooters in the Algiers Point area, gunshot survivors, and those who witnessed bloodshed were later interviewed as well as police officers, forensic pathologists, firefighters, historians, medical doctors and private citizens. More than 800 autopsies were studied and piles of state death records. What emerged was a disturbing picture of New Orleans in the days after the storm when the city fractured along racial fault lines as its government collapsed.

In West Virginia, where roughly 350 people were relocated, local officials took fingerprints to run criminal background checks on the refugees. The background checks found that 45% of the refugees had a criminal record of some nature and that 22% had a violent criminal record. Media speculation fueled a popular perception that the displaced New Orleans residents brought a wave of crime into communities where they relocated; however, detailed studies of crime statistics in these communities did not reveal a significant increase in most areas.

A review of Uniform Crime Report (UCR) data from 2001 to 2010 shows gun violence clearly rose on a per-capita basis in Baton Rouge and Houston in the years following Hurricane Katrina. News agencies carried stories of riots between Houston students and New Orleans students. The rise in gun violence in these other cities was not accompanied by similar rises in other major UCR crimes. While the rise in gun violence in Baton Rouge and Houston following Katrina is fairly striking, that does not prove that the flow of evacuees to those cities alone caused the spike.

Gabe Morales remembers, after Katrina, Seattle, WA, also saw some displaced gang members who claimed "504" after the New Orleans area code. They would often wear camouflaged Hip Hop gear like rapper "Master-P", gold grills and everything. This is also a time period when Seattle started to see some Black gang members gravitate towards "Crunk" music. Custom Highrider cars as often driven by young Blacks in the South were sighted with the most common vehicle 1980s GM sedans or Ford "Crown Vics". In irony, these were the same type often driven as police vehicles, a profession many despised.

Wingate is street in a run down area near the University of New Orleans campus.

504 is the area code for New Orleans

Whatever the public was to believe, there was some effect on nearby cities or even far way ones like Seattle, as well as problems with the rebuilding of New Orleans.

On January 18, 2013, former New Orleans Mayor Ray Nagin was indicted by grand jury on corruption charges including: wire fraud, conspiracy, bribery, money laundering, and filing false tax returns related to bribes from city contractors. On February 20, 2013, Nagin pleaded not guilty in federal court to all charges.

Despite New Orleans' long history of political corruption, Nagin was the first mayor to be criminally charged for corruption in office. He was convicted on 20 of the 21 counts by jury on February 12, 2014. These charges included that he took more than $500,000 in payouts from businessmen in exchange for millions of dollars' worth of city contracts. Law enforcement and other government officials report contracting was shady during the rebuilding period.

Some members of a violent Latino gang, Mara Salvatrucha, were said to have been hired as extra labor and perhaps as cover to get into the country, but there is little hard documentation of this other than MS graffiti on some new structures.

There is hard documentation of other criminal activities in the South.

Some people blamed the fact that many local gang leaders were behind bars as the cause behind much of the violence. Indeed, co-author Adam Schniper notes, "When big sweeps take gang leaders off the streets, it often leaves a vacuum for younger, less disciplined members who want to make a name for themselves. On the streets, you get your reputation through committing violence."

The jailing of high-ranking Chattanooga gang members is at least partially responsible for a wave of violence that swept through city streets in 2016.

Tennessee authorities stated, "Your Chattanooga Police Department and their partnership in fighting gangs is absolutely in the fight, and we're taking the fight to these gangs on the street. It should also tell you that you have criminals in your community and in our community that are so committed to committing violence that they'll do it within sound-shot and sight of police officers."

Not all those who were jailed necessarily pulled the trigger in shootings, but police believe they nabbed the gang leaders who were "calling the shots."

Those gang leaders, according to authorities, have been involved in jail fights that have spilled over to the streets, where lower-tier gang members are jockeying for position to fill the "vacuum" created by the imprisonment of the gang leaders.

The Hamilton County Jail, officials said, was not built to support the number of people it's housing, particularly those who are so violent.

The City of New Orleans was also facing a post-Katrina uptick in violence.

 **Young Melph Mafia Handsigns**

New Orleans' Central City gang member Jacobi Boyd centered less on the 28 grams of crack he was convicted of conspiring to sell and more on the bodies dropped as result of violent turf wars. Boyd was sentenced to serve 40 years in federal prison after pleading guilty to drug and gun charges. Before he handed down Boyd's sentence, U.S. District Judge Kurt Engelhardt and Boyd's attorney Roma Kent talked about the violence Boyd was involved with as a member of Young Melph Mafia, in furtherance of the group's drug dealing network.

In sentencing the 24-year-old Boyd, Engelhardt was allowed to consider the "factual basis" of the drug conspiracy, which included the 2013 murder of 25-year-old Travis Thomas, and other shootings. Thomas was riding in the front passenger seat of a car when he was shot to death May 6, 2013, on I-10 westbound near the Metairie Road exit and the New Orleans Country Club.

Documents containing the facts of the case detailed violence involved in maintaining the operation at the Melpomene Housing Development. It also painted a grim picture of rivalries between multiple warring New Orleans gangs.

What is taught by national experts doesn't always ring 100% true in Alabama.

In Alabama, Pellam PD Officer Adam Schniper believes the biggest, or at least strongest gang in the state, is the Folk Nation, primarily with various branches of the Disciples. While many gang workers say that Folk Nation in Chicago announced recently that all Disciple gangs will fly under one banner, reports in Alabama indicate factions are still claiming IGD, BGD, GD, DDs, etc. Folk Nation groups in Alabama frequently do their own thing and do not pay percentage to Chicago. On the other hand, Mississippi Folk do maintain close ties to the north.

Schniper talks with non-gang and gang affiliated Black prisoners when he can. He hears everything from "the GDs are unorganized in Alabama" up to "they're highly organized with direct contact to Chicago." Both versions may be true depending on the area of the state, but one thing is clear: GDs run Alabama's prison system. Bloods, VLs, Crips, etc., exist under a racial banner, but the GDs run the system, there is no doubt about that.

Some prisoners were never in a Folk gang on the outside, but once on the inside, they join Folk. Schniper has interviewed old school GDs, including one active in the 1980s when they first hit Birmingham. When talking with this first generation GD that he arrested recently, he was told the first GDs in Birmingham were sent from Chicago for a reason. This was not just a fluke occurrence, you could say they were "injected" into Alabama for further expansion, not "imported".

There has been a lot of violence in Birmingham recently. It appears that much of it was "GDs sorting things out". If that is true, law enforcement may not be pinpointing connections fully. According to a reliable source, Crips were the first national gang to hit the Birmingham scene, then next came the GDs, and then the Bloods. It appears that Bloods are more predominant than Crips in the Birmingham area. A Rolling 60's Crip who was arrested in Pelham states he joined the gang in Bessemer, Alabama, at a young age. He's never been to the West Coast. There are neighborhood gangs that affiliate as Crips, but that becomes confusing from a distance since they rep the neighborhood and not so much the Crip affiliation.

Vice Lords are sometimes found in Alabama, but believed to be a lot smaller than the aforementioned gangs. There are also neighborhood and hybrid gangs/money crews. In Pelham, AL, the biggest problem is car break-ins due to money gangs from Birmingham and Bessemer coming in. As soon as one crew is squashed, surviving members just join another crew so it's hard keeping track of them.

According to one state corrections officer, he has observed "Money Gang" members tattooing "MG" on themselves. It's almost as if they claim a generalized idea of being an MG member, but won't actually claim the specific gang set. It is suspected some prisoners don't really know what the future holds as far as what gang or crew they'll be a part of in the future. "Hybrid Gang", in many cases, is a misclassification of a money crew. They often all act the same whether or not they are deemed "legit" by other gangs or law enforcement.

Shelby County, Alabama, located just south of Birmingham, had a huge housing boom occurring back around 2003. Economic prosperity attracted many Latino laborers, primarily being undocumented from Mexico and Central America. Being first generation immigrants, very few actually spoke English Some of their kids joined gangs. Crimes within the community often went unreported.

The problem was so bad that once the local cops had to knock on doors delivering thousands of dollars in stolen jewelry that a burglar confessed to stealing from homes in the area, but no one called the police to report it.

Schniper recalls seeing homeboys standing on corners clockin', (putting in work), but many officers at that time ignored it as they felt there wasn't anything going on. This mainly due to the fact the Latino community wasn't telling anyone.

Schniper, and a few other officers, entered the Latino community to earn some trust. Individuals like Detective Marco Silva from Georgia came and taught Hoover and Pelham PDs about gangs. Trainings were also held in conjunction with groups like the International Latino Gang Investigators Association (ILGIA).

Surenos were often flying their blue rags right in front of police who had no idea what they were looking at or mistook them for Crips. Officers had to learn how about Latino culture and distinguish who was involved in the gang culture. Cops finally started impacting the gang and dope scene in communities and, over time, most folks realized the police were there to go after the bad guys and not them.

This was proved time and time again through law enforcement suppression action, positive field contacts with Latino youth, and community meetings to enhance relations with local law enforcement. At the same time, new Latino community groups were helping people adjust to their new environment and assimilate.

An often rowdy first generation of workers started getting married and having kids. Worker colonies in Alabama transformed into family neighborhoods. Some previously lived in trailers and soon became home owners. Now their kids have kids, so officers know grandparents, parents, and their children.

Anybody teaching on Latino gangs in Alabama, in Schniper's opinion, needs to also include an introduction to the Latino community. Officers need to understand both gangs and what the vast majority of hard working, although sometimes undocumented, Latinos have to go through or police will alienate the good people.

The Gangland episode "Death in Dixie" covers La Gran Familia (LGF). The Arceo family moved to Hoover, Alabama, and then to Pelham. They supposedly moved to their boys away from the Atlanta gang influence. They had two sons who both brought the LGF influence with them. The older brother claimed Malditos (MDS13,a clica attached to Florencia 13 in California), and the younger brother claimed Brown Pride (BP13) which was an affiliate of the other.

Malditos, of course primarily comprised of older individuals, some who also migrated from Atlanta when Malditos began recruiting in the area. Malditos became about twenty strong and BP also had about twenty. BP primarily did the recruiting in local middle schools and also went into high school. Malditos had homies in Tuscaloosa, AL, and Brown Pride had some in Montgomery, AL.

They usually initiated kids with the standard "13 second beat down".

Kids from Homewood, AL, which is located next to Birmingham had been influenced by an older gangster from Kentucky that used to belong to Southside Lokotes (SSL13). So, we now there are Malditos, BP13, and Lokotes active in Shelby County. One of the Lokotes didn't like the way they were run and so he created the Cyclones. This group is primarily a juvenile gang, but nonetheless, another gang attractive to kids in Pelham, Hoover and Alabaster.

Then there is "La Quemada" (LQ). This gang has direct ties to Inglewood 13. LQ operates primarily in a barrio located next to the Birmingham International Airport. It is surrounded by primarily Bloods in a primarily African-American community.

The Inglewood homies that set it all up used to tag SUR 13 in Pelham when they punked our gangs. Then somewhere along the line, they named themselves La Quemada (The Burned). They represent with both LQ13 and ING13 graffiti, just like Malditos used to graffiti LGF. La Quemada has a stepping-stone gang called Youngsters 13. At last study years ago, LQ had a core of maybe twenty members, and the Youngsters possibly 50-75. From Birmingham, they spread into Blount County, NE of Birmingham/Jefferson County.

What made La Quemada stand apart from the other Latino gangs was their direct ties to drug cartels, so they came in hard and did not mess around. Many LQ members Chicano, they were American born thus cannot be deported. Whereas Malditos, BPS, Lokotes, and Cyclones were often not citizens and deported.

Due to deportations, criminal arrests, and fear of LQ, most of the other Latino gangs, with the possible exception of Malditos, have disappeared. It may also be that some of the gang violence has been lowered due to the drug cartel members not wanting younger gangsters to be stupid and bring on heat from the police.

What happened in Alabama was repeated in many Southeast states.

The number of individual gang members within North Carolina's GangNET data base in 2011 totaled 12,845 individuals, with an additional 3,500 inmates bridged from DOC that meet the security threat group validation. The total number of gang members in communities and incarcerated is greater than 15,000.

Almost two-thirds of documented gang members were 21 years of age or older.

The racial makeup of these gangs in 2011 was 8% White, 21% Hispanic, and the vast majority (68%) Blacks with other ethnicities making up a small fraction.

North Carolina has a lot of activity from the United Blood Nation (UBN).

In 2016, two UBN members pled guilty in order to avoid a possible death sentence of killing Debbie and Doug London. The elder couple were killed to prevent them from testifying against two other gang members who had robbed the Londons' store in Pineville, NC.

UBN members conducted a meeting on Oct. 5, 2014, in Greenville, North Carolina. The members had a phone meeting two days later in which they planned the killing of the Londons and "a hit" was ordered on them after two other members failed to kill them, according to court documents. Doug London shot and wounded Jamell Cureton during the attempted robbery of the mattress store.

Cureton, along with another UBN member, was also charged with the 2013 murder of Kwamne Clyburn in Charlotte, NC. According to the indictment, Clyburn was shot to death for "false claiming," gang speak for saying he was a gang member when he was not.

In June 2016, during an attempted murder trial, former members of the Bloods street gang testified that it was normal for a gang leader accused of orchestrating the kidnapping of a Wake County prosecutor's father from prison to run the gang's operations from inside his cell.

UBN gang leader Kelvin Melton was put on trial in federal court in North Carolina for the April 2014 abduction of the father of Assistant District Attorney Colleen Janssen who prosecuted Melton in a 2012 attempted murder in Raleigh, NC, which earned him a life sentence as a habitual felon.

Authorities said Melton used a cellphone smuggled to him in prison to order subordinates to abduct Janssen, but the crew went to the wrong address and grabbed her father by mistake. FBI agents raided an Atlanta apartment and freed Frank Janssen five days after he was kidnapped from his Wake Forest home.

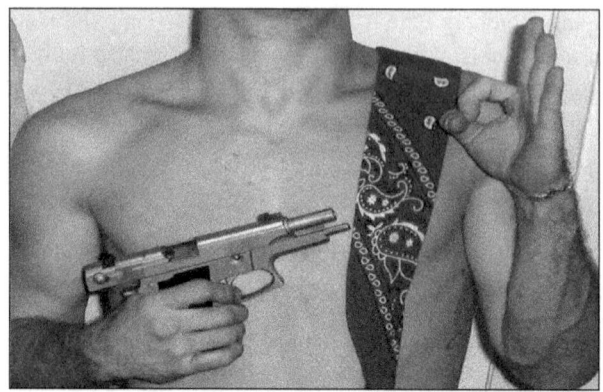 **Blood Handsign**

Central Florida gangs often use social media to recruit new members and promote violence. Furthermore, there frequently is nonconformity from traditional gang knowledge and traditions (i.e. gang colors, style of dress, etc.) that are seen in California, Chicago, and New York. Also, violence between gangs, although they may represent the same umbrella group (like: 59 Brims vs. G-Shine or 8 II Gangster Crip vs. Rolling 30's Crips) often exists.

Because of the lack of structure within the gang and the rapid changing of members there are no accurate official numbers, but the largest single gangs within Central Florida are the Latin Kings and Amigo De Nadie (ADN). However, if you place all the different sets of the Bloods from Central Florida into one group they become the most dominate group in the region.

The drug trade is a large influence for the gangs in Florida as most of them have combined their efforts with the cartels and other drug trafficking organizations. Recently, juveniles sets of gangs have been committing most of our grab and dash operations within the retail sectors and gun shops.

Since 2006, about 90% percent of the murders, batteries and assaults committed within the Central Florida area were committed by documented gang members or their associates. Recently, law enforcement has been the targeted by gang. The 59 Brims put multiple hits out on officers and their families. They have also damaged property belonging to patrol officer and corrections officers as retaliation from them getting involved in their affairs. These groups continue to be monitored.

Haitian Gangs

Zoe Pound is a criminal street gang based in Miami, Florida, founded by Haitian immigrants. Zoe is the anglicized variant of the word *Zo*, which is Haitian Creole to mean *bone,* whose members were known to be "hard to the bone." When conflicts against Haitians arose, the *pound* would be sought out to retaliate, thus the street gang name, Zoe Pound came to be.

Having branched out from Miami in the two decades leading up to 2010, they are known to be involved in drug trafficking and robbery and related violent crimes in support of their drug trafficking activities in other areas such as Indiana.

In 2009, six Zoe Pound leaders were arrested on racketeering and conspiracy charges in Fort Pierce, Florida after Florida Department of Law Enforcement offices convinced several gang members to give testimony for the prosecution.

One fallacy that a lot of people have, not all Whites join Supremacist groups. Many times they are accepted by Crips of Gangster Disciples and will be even more "down" than a Black gang members might be that make up the majority. While these White members are often looked at with affection by minority gang members, they often have trouble with Aryans who view them as being traitors.

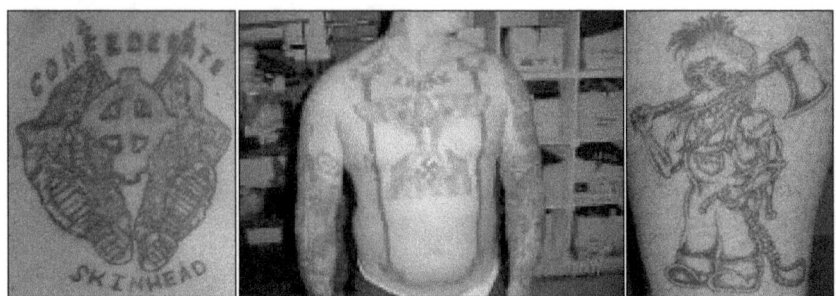

With 20 active hate groups and just under 3 million residents, Arkansas is home to the second highest ratio of hate groups per million residents in the country. In the city of Harrison alone, there are four distinct Ku Klux Klan chapters, including Knights of the KKK and Knights Party Veterans League. There appears to be a relationship between poor rates of educational attainment and the presence of racist groups. Just over 20% of Arkansas residents have a bachelor's degree or higher, the third lowest rate in the country.

The Aryan Nations Knights and the Loyal White Knights are active in Louisiana as factions of the KKK. Tennessee hate groups include Ku Klux Klan branches such as the Southern Mountain Knights, the Original Knight Riders Knights, and the Loyal White Knights, as well as neo-Nazi groups such as the Creativity Alliance and the Aryan Nations.

In addition to Latino and Black gangs, Skinheads, Peckerwoods, and Aryan groups are alive and well in the Deep South. In fact, these gangs have replaced much of the activity traditionally done by racist groups like the KKK.

The State of Alabama has Confederate Hammer Skins primarily and they are also active in South Carolina.

With a population of 3 million and 22 active hate groups, Mississippi has the highest concentration of hate groups in the country. Poorly educated populations are among the most likely to participate in hate groups. Only 20.4% of adults in the state have a bachelor's degree or higher, the second smallest share in the U.S. The Council of Conservative Citizens, a White nationalist group, has chapters in four cities across the state, while the Black Separatist group Nation of Islam has chapters in three.

While Sovereign Citizens are not considered a street gang, they can definitely be disruptive.

According to the Federal Bureau of Investigation, "Sovereign Citizens are anti-government extremists who believe that even though they physically reside in this country, they are separate or "sovereign" from the United States. As a result, they believe they don't have to answer to any government authority, including courts, taxing entities, motor vehicle departments, or law enforcement."

Sovereign Citizen Ideology believe laws do not apply to them and they have blatant disregard for authority. This makes them a high risk encounter whenever approached by law enforcement and there is growing concern for their activities once they enter jail and prison systems. In some facilities they are considered part of a Security Threat Group (STG).

While incarcerated, inmates often look for like-minded individuals that believe in similar ideologies, religions, and politics. Therefore, it is common for incarcerated individuals, who often already hold contempt for authority, to be exposed to Sovereign teachings and adopt them.

While incarcerated, Sovereign Citizens are known to file endless grievances, cease and desist orders against staff, "warrants" on staff, and questioning and arguing in disciplinary hearings much the same as they have been known to do in court prior to being incarcerated. Other inmates see these actions and begin studying Sovereign teachings for the sole purpose of making life difficult for prison staff.

Many states have seen validated Security Threat Group members beginning to study Sovereign teachings and incorporate them into their gang lifestyle. Gang members are using the guise of Sovereign teachings as a religion and as justification for their anti-authority actions. In at least one case in North Carolina, a Sovereign Citizen helped incite a riot and assaults on staff, carried out by gang members, by shouting his anti-authority rhetoric in order to boost other inmates and justify their actions.

Even though Sovereign Citizens have been traditionally nothing more than the sporadic individual who has extremist views, it is becoming more common in the correctional setting that inmates who possess Sovereign ideologies are starting to group themselves under the auspices of "religion".

In particular, inmates have been reported to claim being part of "The Moorish American Government", which inmates claim makes them exempt from U.S. laws.

They hide their teachings and ideologies under the cover of the "Moorish Science Temple of America", which in many states is a recognized religion.

On July 17, 2016, Gavin Eugene Long shot six police officers in Baton Rouge, LA. Three died and three were hospitalized, one critically; of the officers who died, two were members of the Baton Rouge Police Department, while the third worked for the East Baton Rouge Parish Sheriff's Office. Long, who was a former Marine Corps Sgt., associated himself with organizations linked to Black separatism and the Moorish Science Temple of America.

The Nation of Islam based in Birmingham, AL, with other chapters all over the U.S., is considered a hate group by the Southern Poverty Law Center.

In addition, 5 %ers, also known as the Nation of Gods and Earths, is a big problem in places like South Carolina. They say they are a religion, but many agencies define them as a Security Threat Group.

Gang members, estimated at possibly 40,000, are involved in more than 50 percent of the violent crime in Atlanta, according to Jim Hurley, Supervisor for the Atlanta Safe Streets Gang Task Force.

As predicted by many, Latino gangs are gaining influence in the area.

In 2016, federal Agents in Georgia seized more than $800,000 in methamphetamine, $20,000 in cocaine and $12,000 in marijuana in March, dubbing the drug ring the "Lenox Park Cartel" because virtually every single one of the people arrested lived in the Lenox Park subdivision or knew people who did.

In the previous ten years, multiple violent disputes occurred between two local street gangs La Onda ("The Happening" in Spanish slang) and SUR-13 (generic umbrella gang, in theory, claiming loyalty to the Mexican Mafia).

Georgia is no stranger to Mexican drug cartel activity, as one of the largest US-based methamphetamine labs controlled by La Familia Michoacana was discovered in Gwinnett County. Another bust came in late November 2015 as investigators arrested 26 individuals and shut down a drug ring with cartel ties.

David Maldonado Baza, known as "Chucky", was the main supplier and target of the operation. Once they arrested Chucky, drug availability on the street decreased; however, not for long. The cartels usually quickly find another person to take their place to meet the demand and supply side that make the drug business so lucrative.

La Gran Familia Bust

Latino gangs in Alabama come from all over. In the past, the state's biggest threat was gangs that migrated from Atlanta, specifically Malditos 13, which was connected to Georgia La Gran Familia conglomerate. That threat has waned. The most serious gang back then, and probably still now, in Central Alabama is LQ-La Quemada (The Burned). LQ was imported from Inglewood, CA, in the form of Inglewood 13. They maintained their Inglewood heritage as was observed in their graffiti and social site postings. They engaged in drug trafficking, warehousing contraband, money protection, stolen new and high quality firearms, prostitution, gang-on-gang assaults, and murders. They were suspected of, although not fully documented, having cartel connections.

LQ is the last man standing right now, but laying low. Their numbers were last documented at around 20, but a sub-gang, called the Youngsters was boasting nearly 100 at one time. Like much of America, information received throughout the years lends local law enforcement to believe the Cartels have quieted the street gangs so as not to draw attention to their large money making operations.

In 2016, twenty-three people, arrested a crackdown on South Florida's violent Latin Kings gang, pled guilty to a variety of federal charges. The top-ranking gang member caught in the roundup was 36-year-old Christopher Isabel who faced 20 years in prison after pleading guilty to racketeering. Prosecutors said he was the second highest ranking Latin King leader in the State of Florida.

Sources:

Drug Supermarket with Mexican Cartel Ties Busted in Georgia, (AP) 12/3/15

Gang members charged 2014 Lake Wylie murders, Charlotte Observer, 4/22/15

Gavin Long: Who is Baton Rouge cop killer?, CNN, 8/4/16

Gang and Security Threat Group Awareness, Florida DOC Website, 2016

Sovereign Citizens, Chris Rich, G-Force Magazine, Sept-Oct. 2015

Gang Report, Gwinnett County SO, 2015

Despite history of gangs, arrests, some north Ga. residents feel safe, Atlanta Journal-Constitution, 5/1/16

Gang Report, Louisiana Gang Investigator's Association, Sept. 2000

Gang Report, Miami-Dade PD, 2015

Post-Katrina, White Vigilantes Shot African-Americans, The Nation, 1/5/09

Gangs in North Carolina: An Analysis of GangNET Data, NC Governor's Crime Commission, 8/9/11

Gang Report, New Orleans PD, 2015

Gang Report, Adam Schniper, 2016

Gang Report, South Carolina-DOC, 2016

New Orleans Street Gang War, Times Free Press 10/11/16

Chattanooga Gang War, The Times-Picayune, 12/9/15

Ray Nagin, once New Orleans' mayor, now federal inmate No. 32751-034, The Times Picayne, 9/8/14

Magic City: Trials of a Native Son, Trick Daddy and Peter Bailey, 2010

Officers prepare for gangs to emerge, Tuscaloosa News, 4/16/10

Investigating Gangs in Louisville, WDRB-TV, 5/10/16

Gangs continue to grow, cause problems in central Florida, WFTV, 11/5/13

Henchmen: Gang leader called all shots from prison, WRAL, 6/9/16

Gangs in Southeastern Jails and Prisons

Gangs have been active in southern state prisons for over a century and a half.

In February 1864, during the Civil War, a Confederate prison was established in Macon County, in southwest Georgia. It provided relief for the large number of Union prisoners concentrated in and around Richmond, Virginia. The new camp, officially named Camp Sumter, quickly became known as Andersonville, named after the railroad station in a neighboring county close to where the camp was located. By the summer of 1864, the camp held the largest prison population of its time, with numbers that would have made it the fifth-largest city in the Confederacy. By the time it closed in early May 1865, those numbers, along with the sanitation, health, and mortality problems stemming from its overcrowding, earned Andersonville a reputation as one of the most notorious Confederate atrocities inflicted on Union troops.

Andersonville had the highest mortality rate of any Civil War prison. Nearly 13,000 of the 45,000 men who entered the stockade eventually died there, chiefly of malnutrition.

Camp inmates often preyed upon each other. Gambling tents and "stores," operated mainly by prisoners from Union General William T. Sherman's western troops, fleeced new arrivals. Roving gangs of raiders, chiefly from eastern regiments, robbed fellow inmates, despite efforts by guards to stop them. The prisoners hanged six of the raider leaders on July 11, 1864. After that, a new police force made up of prisoners sought to impose discipline on their fellow inmates.

Today, these prison groups are often made up of individuals who met out on the streets and did business together. When they were tried, convicted, and locked up for their crimes, many continue a life of crime behind the walls.

There are no know homegrown prison gangs that started in southern prison systems before the 1970s even though convict "bulls" existed in the fashion previously described, thus, these groups were not classified as homegrown "prison gangs". Up until the 1970s really, southern institutions were run by the strongest and most manipulate prisoners in a "inmate straw boss" system.

A good depiction of this scheme was portrayed in the fictitious movie "Cool Hand Luke" (1967) starring Paul Newman as a defiant prisoner named Luke and in the semi-nonfiction movie "Brubaker" (1980) starring Robert Redford as a prison warden who goes undercover to stamp out abuse and corruption.

Prison gangs threaten the safe and secure operations of the prison facilities. Prison investigators try to identify these individuals, disrupt their activities that are in violation of policy and/or state law, and work to establish ways to track the individuals, groups, and their activities. Inside the facilities gang activity accounts for a significant number of serious assaults and batteries.

Gangs in prison often rely on technology to stay connected to their counterparts and to help drive their illicit activities. This is particularly true for prison gangs that seek to obtain cell phones in order to access the outside world. Cell phones and social media platforms enable fast communication and coordination efforts among street gang members; between gang members in prison; and between prison and street members. In all of these instances, communication serves to enhance criminal operations and further gang objectives.

The Mississippi Department of Corrections confiscated 2,257 cell phones across three prisons between the beginning of 2013 and April 2014. The department implemented a variety of preventive measures to reduce the number of cell phones in prisons, such as weekly searches for WiFi Internet signals; installing netting around prison perimeters; and increased searches using Managed Access Systems, Boss Chairs "body cavity detection systems," K-9 cell phone detector dogs, hand-wand metal detectors, and walk-through metal detection systems.

Other states face similar problems dealing with gangs in jails and prisons.

Alabama

There are two identified prison gangs in the state, the Aryan Brotherhood of Alabama and the Southern Brotherhood (SB of Alabama) that was formed in 1995. SB also has a motorcycle club on the street that uses "DOC" (Department of Corrections) a bottom rocker. Aryan Skinhead gangs go back in the late 80's and early 90's. The Skinhead Movement waned, as it did nationwide, Alabama has Confederate Hammer Skins primarily, but at one time did have White Aryan Resistance (WAR) Skins.

As mentioned earlier, after numerous gang and prisoner interviews, it appears Folk Nation gangs out on the streets in Alabama do not pay a percentage or taxes to Chicago. Some older GDs claim Brothers of the Struggle (BOS). The GD Governor for Alabama for the federal system is known as "T-Man".

Arkansas

According to a Deputy Warden and Security Threat Group Coordinator with the Arkansas Department of Corrections, "Prison gangs threaten the safe and secure operations of the prison facilities. Our efforts work to identify these individuals, disrupt their activities that are in violation of policy and/or state law, and work to establish ways to track the individuals, groups, and their activities." Deputy Warden Aiken and AR-DOC has identified Gangster Disciplines (Folks), Bloods, and Aryan/Supreme White Power groups as being the largest within the system.

According to the ADL, the Aryan Circle is active in the state.

The New Aryan Empire (NAE) started in the state in the 1990s.

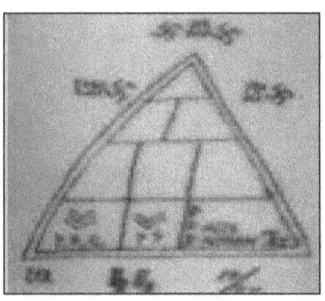

White Aryan Resistance (WAR) of Arkansas

The White Aryan Resistance (WAR) is a large, Arkansas-based white supremacist prison gang. They borrowed their name from California white supremacist Tom Metzger, who invented it in the 1980s for his own group. The main symbol of the Arkansas gang is an elaborate pyramid tattoo divided into nine "bricks." Gang members are allowed to fill in the "bricks" of the tattoo with rank symbols as they achieve them. One "brick" also usually contains the runic lettering for "skinhead" and the numeric symbol 14/88.

Outside the pyramid, the WAR tattoo features the initials WAR, each letter accompanied by swastikas. Runic letters for "WAR", SS lightning bolts, and the numeric symbol 14/88 will often appear below the pyramid.

These groups are involved in various prison contraband trades such as smuggling in cell phones, drugs and tobacco, extortion and fraud. They also account for a significant number of serious assaults and batteries.

Gangster Disciplines (Folks) and Bloods are also active in the Arkansas prison system. These gangs are involved in various prison contraband trades (May not be criminal items such as cell phones and tobacco), extortion, fraud, etc.

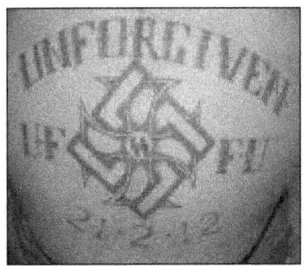

Florida Prison Gangs

According the Florida Department of Corrections, Ñetas, Latin Kings, and Aryan Brotherhood are all active in their system. Unforgiven is a prison gang started in the state in 1986 and according to the ADL is the largest Aryan gang in the system. Their main symbol consists of an interlocking Iron Cross and swastika, with SS lightning bolts in the center. Gang members will also often use the numeric code 21-2-12. Bloods in Florida-DOC are organizing under the banner of the United Blood Nation (UBN). Gangster Disciples are also active, the GD Gov. is "Kuntry".

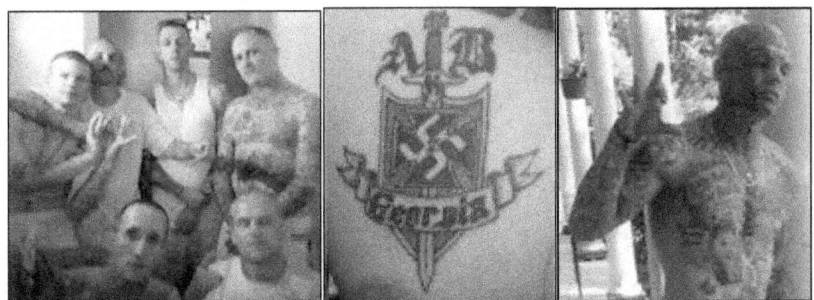

Prison Recruitment in Georgia

The Georgia Aryan Brotherhood is quite active in the state. Another prison gang is the Ghost Face Gangsters (GFG) which were brought to the state by a California GFG member. They are believed to have around 3,000 members in the U.S.

According to March 2015 open source reporting, a photo taken inside of a Georgia correctional facility showing a badly beaten inmate with a leash around his neck was uploaded to Facebook. The caption on the photo read, *"When you disrespect the Nation, it brings nothing but pain and suffering"*.

Cortez Berry was turning 18 Saturday, and about a dozen of his friends at the Burruss Correctional Training Center in Forsyth, Ga., wanted to give him a present.

"The (Gangster Disciples) came in and told him that since he was turning 18, he might as well join the gang, because you about to go to the other side," said Berry's aunt Shavondria Wright of Jonesboro.

According to Wright, Berry refused the invitation. At that point, about 10 gang members savagely beat and humiliated Berry, who is serving an eight-year term for armed robbery and carjacking.

By prison standards, the beating might have been considered routine. But what happened next vividly exposed the nature of prison, the ways of gangs and the never-ending struggle to control the smuggling of contraband such as cell phones.

The aftermath of the attack on Berry was photographed and uploaded to Facebook.

Hundreds of thousands of people gazed upon Berry's defeated eyes as he was forced to kneel before two of his victors with a makeshift leash around his neck.

Online, reaction to the attack has ranged from sympathy to apathy.

Gwendolyn Hogan, a spokesperson for the Georgia Department of Corrections, said the department is still investigating the photograph and the circumstances surrounding it. She would not comment on Wright's claim that Berry was beaten for declining to join a gang.

Wright said she was at the prison checking on her nephew within hours of the photo being posted. When she arrived, she said, many of the guards didn't even realize what happened to him.

"And I haven't heard anything from the prison since," Wright said. "I don't even think they sent him out for medical attention yet."

Wright, who visits Berry regularly because of her proximity to the prison, said she was shocked when she saw his condition. Berry, she said, was terrified and embarrassed that his image is now plastered across social media. Tuesday, Wright provided the Atlanta Journal-Constitution with a second photograph taken after the beating, which has not been aired publicly.

"He isn't going to admit it, but deep down in his mind, he has to be fearful that something else can happen," Wright said. "And for me, I can't sleep at night, because I don't know if my nephew is safe."

Since 2010, one corrections officer and 33 prisoners have been killed in Georgia prisons.

According to a study released by the Southern Center for Human Rights, gangs dominate Georgia's prison system, the nation's fourth largest.

"Gangs control inmate housing assignments and expel inmates they no longer want in their dorms," the report said. "Gangs pose a formidable challenge to prison security even in well-run prisons. In prisons where security is neglected, gangs step in to perform functions that prison officials fail to perform."

The report also suggests that rising violence in Georgia prisons stems partly from prisoners having access to illegal contraband, particularly cell phones, which are used to coordinate and commit crimes, as well as to carry out extortion.

"Cell phones are often used to commit and plan crimes outside of prison, but also to incite violence and to extort family members of those who are incarcerated," said Sarah Geraghty, a senior attorney with the organization. "We hear from family members all the time that they will receive a text picture of their loved ones, who have been beaten, with the message: 'Pay us money or something will happen.'

In 2012, the AJC reported that corrections officials confiscated more than 8,700 illegal cell phones the year before. A year later, NBC News reported that 13,500 cell phones were confiscated.

"First and foremost, the Department (of Corrections) does not tolerate contraband and takes very seriously its mission of protecting the public and running safe and secure facilities," Hogan said. She said the prison system has bought and installed a variety of devices to help prison officials detect contraband cell phones and other electronics.

"It is hard to see (the image of Berry) on the Internet," Wright said. "But in this situation, I am kind of grateful that they had contraband, or we wouldn't have known about this."

While Hogan would not comment on the incident, Wright said the last time she spoke Berry, he told her that he was in protective custody. She said she is not sure of his current status.

Berry has been in the system since at least 2011, when, at the age of 14, he was sent to the Richmond County Youth Detention Center after being charged with armed robbery and carjacking in Augusta.

His current stint at Burruss started March 31, 2014, when he was charged with a parole violation.

"He is a kind-hearted person, who did a bad thing in the past. He made a mistake," Wright said. "But I see him maturing more as a man. He said when he gets out, he is going to find a job and make better decisions. He always tells my oldest that he doesn't want to end up in there with him."

Louisiana

The Louisiana State Penitentiary has been home to many Dixie Mafia members. Gangster Disciples are active in the state and when sentenced to prison can cause problems in custody. The GD Federal Governor is known as "Chevy". The Aryan Circle is a large, growing and dangerous white supremacist prison gang based primarily in Texas, though it has a presence in a number of other states. It is active both in prisons and on the streets. It is an extreme and violent group, with a long track record of murder, including the deaths of two police officers in Bastrop, Louisiana, in 2007.

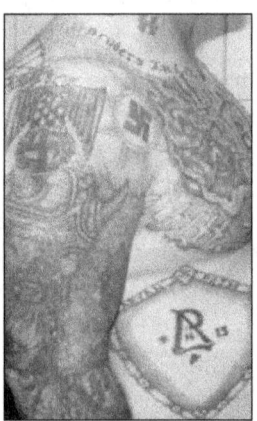

Mississippi

The Aryan Brotherhood originally was a California-based prison gang, formed in the 1960s, which later branched out nationwide, with copycat autonomous branches in virtually every state in the nation, including Mississippi. The Aryan Brotherhood of Mississippi (ABM) members was started in 1984. AMB members often get a "13" tattoo for the 13th letter (M) in the alphabet. (This is not to be confused with the Mexican Mafia who often direct subordinates called Surenos who often get 13 tattoos to show support for La EME). The ABM operates in and out of prisons in the state. Authorities say the ABM is linked to racketeering, illegal drug trafficking, kidnappings, murders and other federal crimes.

The ABM was founded in 1984, modeled after the precepts and writings of the Aryan Brotherhood of California (founded in 1967). In early 2013, the leadership of the ABM began efforts to unify with the Aryan Brotherhood of California in order to achieve national recognition, authorities say.

The state was overseen and directed by a three-member "wheel" commonly referred to as "spokes," according to federal investigators. During the times alleged, the wheel of the ABM was comprised of "spokes" Frank "State Raised" Owens Jr., 44, of D'Iberville, Miss.; Perry Mask, 46, of Corinth, Miss.; Steven Hubanks, 45, of Rienzi, Miss.; and Brandon "Oak" Creel, 46, of Ellisville, Miss. Owens and Eric Glenn Parker, 35, of Richton, Miss., were convicted April 13, 2016, by a federal jury in Aberdeen, Miss., of engaging in a racketeering conspiracy and murder.

A captain in the Aryan Brotherhood of Mississippi fronted Michael "Skip" Hudson $250 worth of methamphetamine, but he and another member of the gang didn't like the quality so they refused to pay for it. One of the Brotherhood's statewide leaders ordered the dispute settled with "minutes," meaning a fistfight, a common method of conflict resolution within the highly organized and hierarchical gang. But Hudson refused to show and it cost him his life.

When Frankie "State Raised" Owens Jr. heard an ABM soldier ignored a direct command, he waited for Hudson with three other members at one of their trailers, close to the Alabama border. When a gang soldier and a recruit arrived with Hudson in December 2010, having lured him on Owens's orders by lying that they were on their way to cook meth, the full fury of the prison gang was unleashed.

Owens used a billy club he nicknamed "Blackie" as he and the five other men beat Hudson. They then bound him with wire and loaded him into the trunk of a car for a 90-mile drive north to meet with Eric Parker, the captain who had given Hudson the meth. When they arrived at Parker's trailer, he wasn't home, so Owens let Hudson out of the trunk and allowed him to smoke a cigarette. When Parker arrived a few minutes later, he and Owens strangled Hudson with a baseball bat, court papers state.

Later that night, Parker frantically called the gang's highest-ranking leader outside prison, Brandon "Oak" Creel, to say things had gotten out of hand and they needed help. Owens and Parker then tossed Hudson's body in the back of a pickup truck and drove to Creel's house where they wrapped the body in carpet and stuffed it into a 55-gallon drum. Creel used a backhoe to dig a pit, lined it with roofing metal and put the drum inside. He then tossed in tires, doused them with gasoline and sparked up a tire fire that he kept burning for five days. Finally, he folded up the roofing metal that lined the pit and dumped his homemade crematorium into a nearby creek.

Hudson's brutal murder and elaborate burial were the centerpiece of a federal indictment that convicted forty-two Aryan Brotherhood of Mississippi members and associates and halted the gang's plan to consolidate with the national Aryan Brotherhood. Recent prosecutions in Texas and Oklahoma show that, just like in Mississippi, local Aryan Brotherhood groups kept those states flooded with methamphetamine while enforcing a brutal "blood in, blood out" loyalty both in prison and in what they call the "free world."

The Mississippi AB calls itself "the Family" and is ruled by a three-man "Wheel" that divides the state into nine zones. The Wheel appoints a captain to oversee each zone and prison, with a network of sergeants-at-arms who enforce order and discipline, a treasurer to handle finances and numerous soldiers. Recruits are in "prospect status" for six months before they can be assigned a "blood in mission," like the one assigned to the prospective member who helped lure Hudson to his death. The day Hudson was beaten, the new recruit that was present received his "brand," or tattoo, signifying full membership in the gang.

The ABM Constitution also lays out the gang's ideology: "We are the elite few of our race who have been selected for the sacred mission of preserving our purity and supremacy in these rapidly changing times," the document states, tracing the gang's lineage to the Ku Klux Klan. "Are Africans, Jews, or Asians equal to the Aryans of pure white stock? No!" But strict adherence to Aryan ideology and racism is uneven, law enforcement officials say. While some members are "true believers," others simply get a few Nazi-inspired tattoos and parrot the Aryan creed to obtain protection in prison and lucrative criminal opportunities on the outside.

In April 2016, a federal jury in the Northern District of Mississippi convicted two members of the Aryan Brotherhood of Mississippi gang for their participation in various criminal acts, including racketeering, conspiracy, methamphetamine production and trafficking, kidnapping, murder and other federal offenses, ending a two-and-a-half-year investigation and prosecution which resulted in the convictions of 42 members and associates of the gang.

North Carolina

Peer pressure can be extremely hard to fight in jail and prisons. The North Carolina Department of Public Safety says gangs have threatened and attacking correctional officers if they don't get what they want. The Aryan Brotherhood of North Carolina often calls the shots for White inmates. Bound for Glory (BFG) was started in 2001, was founded with approval from the Supreme White Alliance (SWA). The East Coast version of United Blood Nation (UBN) is also very active. Crips and various SUR13 gangs are also active in the prison system.

The Federal Gangster Disciple Governor for the state is known as "Ski Man". According to North Carolina's GangNET data base in 2011, approximately 3,500 inmates met their security threat group validation criteria. North Carolina continues to be a hotbed for prison gang activity.

South Carolina

A corrections officer at the South Carolina Department of Juvenile Justice says gangs are strong inside the youth prison, which has led to at least three riots from 2015-16. C/O Catherine McKnight told a House committee investigating problems at DJJ that if the things don't improve children and staffers could be killed.

DJJ officials say a disturbance on February 26, 2016, started when several juveniles jumped a rival gang leader during a Black History Month ceremony. Five juveniles have been charged as adults for their roles in the riot. Officials say one inmate started a fire, and then at least two others broke into a girls' dorm and tried to sexually assault some of the girls there. Officials say the juveniles broke windows, tore sinks off the walls, damaged vehicles outside, and one juvenile got into a vehicle and tried to run over someone.

DJJ Director Sylvia Murray told lawmakers that the agency hasn't had a police chief in almost three years and hasn't had a gang intervention specialist in a year. But she says DJJ is taking steps to better protect prisoners and staff, including implementing stricter discipline, installing sinks that can't be ripped from walls, and housing juveniles based on risk.

South Carolina's gangs look different today and are focusing more on white collar crime like tax fraud and human trafficking, experts say. Gangs are domestic terrorists both out on streets and in prisons, said Capt. Vincent Goggins, a Richland County deputy who heads the Midlands Gang Task Force.

That's why law enforcement officers at the conference emphasized knowing each other so that when a new case or trend emerges, investigators know who to call, said former South Carolina Department of Corrections gang expert Elbert Pearson.

"Now has come the time where since we have gangs in every community, what can we do about it?" Pearson said. "When you network with people, they know a familiar voice and a familiar name. Then they'll give stuff to you easily."

Tennessee Prison System

Dirty White Boys (DWB), often a farm team for federal Aryan Brotherhood members, is also sometimes seen within the state of Tennessee with a state patch.

The Aryan Brotherhood of Tennessee often states "Brotherhood Forever" alluding to the blood in, blood out lifetime rule. Per the founder, the group was started in 1994. He originally wanted to call the group Aryan Brotherhood Forever, but the Aryan Brotherhood of Texas (ABT) would not approve it, but did allow Brotherhood Forever. The Aryan Brotherhood is said not to recognize the Brotherhood Forever as affiliate today.

The original intent for the group was based on "religion." Additional sponsorship for the group was sought and received by the founder from CJCC. The sponsor was none other than Aryan Nations (AN) founder Richard Butler. Brotherhood Forever differed from the AN ideology, which the founder say was "more political based."

The difference between the Aryan Brotherhood and Brotherhood Forever is that AB is derived "more on preservation of race with a mixture of politics."

Aryan Nations of Tennessee

The largest white supremacist prison gang in Tennessee calls itself Aryan Nations. The Aryan Nations has repeatedly stated it is not a prison gang, but Tennessee reports it is the largest Security Threat group with over 700 members. The gang borrowed its title from the older neo-Nazi group of the same name, though the two are separate groups with few connections. The "gang" Aryan Nations is also far larger than the "neo-Nazi" Aryan Nations. The main symbol for this racist prison gang consists of a rounded Celtic Cross image with different symbols in each of the quadrants formed by the circle and the cross. These can include the initials AN, the number 14/88, SS lightning bolts, prison bars, stars from the Confederate flag, swastikas, and other symbols. Gang members may also use other symbols, such as the numeric symbol 114 (substituting letters for numbers, 114 equates to A and N, or Aryan Nations).

Prisons play a central role in the gang problem in Tennessee. Gangs are recruiting from behind bars every day with 12 percent of inmates confirmed gang members and another 10 percent suspected.

The state collects information on gang members coming into the system, including photographing their tattoos. They isolate the worst gang offenders from the general population to try to cut down on recruiting. In recent years, the department has started programs to give inmates who want out a chance to renounce their membership from gangs.

"I wish I could say we could control it or stop it," former Correction Commissioner George Little said in an interview before leaving the post in December. "We manage it." The problem is a public safety concern because of weak state sentencing laws that allow serious and violent offenders to be eligible for parole after serving 30 percent of their time, police say. And gangs pose a threat to guards and other inmates while behind bars.

Smuggled Cell Phones in TN-DOC

In 2005, a Gangster Disciple inmate, George Hyatte, used a cell phone smuggled in to coordinate his escape. It resulted in the death of Correction Officer Wayne Morgan.

In a recent case, an inmate who had access to various sections of the prison was resisting a gang's pressure to traffic drugs. Gang members used cell phones to get one of their associates on the outside to go to the inmate's mother's house. A picture taken at the mother's house was sent back to the prisoners via cell phone text message. It was intended to intimidate the inmate.

The problem is also exacerbated by the corruption of correctional officers. A third of all recorded attempts to bribe or solicit prison staff came from gang members, a correction report found. Assault among inmates occurs at a higher rate among gang-affiliated inmates than non-affiliated inmates, particularly assaults involving injury, the report said.

Sources:

Communiqué, Arkansas DOC, Dec. 3, 2015

Gang rites may have sparked viral prison beating, Atlanta Journal Const, 3/31/15

White supremacist gang member arrested, Charlotte Observer, 12/8/16

Andersonville Prison, Robert Scott Davis, 1/21/03

Gang and Security Threat Group Awareness, Florida DOC Website, 2016

Prison Gangs in America, Gabriel Morales, 2008, Revised 2015

Brutal Murder Busts Up Aryan Brotherhood of Mississippi, Newsweek, 6/22/16

Biloxi's Tale of Murder, Extortion and Racy Photos, New York Times, 12/21/91

Gang Report, North Carolina-DOC, 2016

Gangs in North Carolina: An Analysis of GangNET Data, North Carolina Governor's Crime Commission, 8/9/11

Southern Poverty Law Center, 2016, SPLC Website

Cool Hand Luke, Stuart Rosenburg, Warner Bros., 1967

SC gangs evolving, switching to white collar crime, The State, 8/8/16

Brubaker Stuart, Rosenburg, 20th Century Fox, 1980

Tennessee Prison Gangs, The Tennessean, 2011

Gangs are strong in SC's juvenile prison, WSPA-TV, 3/11/16

Closing

Impact on the Community

New gangs continue to emerge in the Southeast U.S. area. Some have little in common with national groups, these local groups often thrive out on the street. They are often made up of youngsters who don't want a lot of discipline or rules that often come with large national groups. They don't have to pay taxes and they don't have to listen to any Big Homies bossing them around.

In Tennessee, Hamilton County Juvenile Court Judge Robert Philyaw chooses his words carefully because he is not allowed to discuss publicly the details of cases involving juveniles. "They sit in my courtroom a few just have this blank look of indifference," he said. The particular young man in question had committed a crime that would be serious even for an adult. But he showed no concern for his actions or his situation. "The kids we see, by the time we get them on a delinquency matter at age 13 or 15 or 16, many of them are hardened," Philyaw said in his conference room at the juvenile court offices on East Third Street. "They have lived through some hard times."

For gang members, in particular, the judge said he senses a feeling of helplessness and hopelessness. "A feeling of hopelessness that they're never going to make it to age 19," he said. "They're not going to be able to get out of this cycle of poverty and things. And helplessness, because they don't know how, they have no male figures in their lives for the most part."

Most of the teens in his courtroom are suffering from some form of mental or emotional problem, he said.

Volunteer Behavioral Health, which runs the Johnson Mental Health Center in Chattanooga, TN, recently won a five-year grant from the state to help troubled teens find mental health resources, and here locally it has decided to make gang members a main focus.

Grant outreach coordinator Knetta Jones said her first task is to get teens to see the mental health services as something they need. "We don't want them to feel like they have to break apart from the gang, but to seek out services that will eventually help them leave the gang," she said. Teens don't want to admit they have mental health problems. "They feel stigmatized it's not a popular diagnosis," Jones said. "We will try to bridge the gap."

Philyaw said he believes teens with mental problems are very susceptible to gangs.

"These kids are labeled early on either as slow or otherwise troublemakers and put in Special Ed. And if they don't get help or are not shown how they can succeed and get over these hurdles, many times they end up getting to a level where they get suspended and expelled and fall off the rolls and quit going to school. The gangs are there to welcome them in."

Marquitta Brown is a detective in the (GPD) Gainesville Police Department's Gang Unit in Florida where she strives to keep more kids from dying. She remembers growing up in the area as they did. "I was living in that type of environment where people were getting shot and killed. Four or five days before graduation we lost about three classmates to gunfire," Brown said. "I'm very, very passionate about being a police officer first and foremost, but even before I became a police officer, my passion was working with youth."

Some disgruntlement over the emphasis on youth programs is evident at GPD. Some see measures such as not arresting kids at school for relatively minor disruptions on campus as too coddling and examples of a "hug-a-thug" approach.

But others believe the programs prevent crime, save officers the time of having to respond to calls involving kids and crime, and change the path of a child's life.

Programs include summer Heatwave of teen basketball, pool parties and a lounge at the Martin Luther King Center; HEROES, in which kids who have run afoul of the law learn skills to find jobs, to treat others with respect and to gain responsibility for their actions; and BOLD, which does much of the same for older teens and young adults.

Louis Guiden grew up on the streets of Shreveport, Louisiana. He moved to the Seattle, WA, area with a cousin to get away from his environment. He quickly became entangled in street life in his new home.

He soon became enlightened about his predicament and now mentors youth.

GuidenU4Life is a human services provider which employs prevention and intervention strategies to develop services which educate undeserved individuals, groups, families and communities of color. The goal of GuidenU4Life is to empower people within communities of color to live more satisfying, autonomous, and productive lives, through the utilization of increased knowledge, tangible resources, and, healthy, productive relationships.GuidenU4Life incorporates the human services practice model to assess and deliver services. This model views people, service and the social environment as integrated entities. This perspective helps individuals, families and communities address and overcome issues and barriers that arise from a variety of social problems and adverse societal conditions.

Louis also runs the Good Shepherd Youth Outreach program. Known for his "realness" and "get-to-the-root-of-the-matter" approach, Mr. Guiden has a passion for learning and development and is a relevant messenger in challenging times, bringing an empowering, life changing message that calls the listener to action, ignites one's core, and activates change. In 2008, Louis successfully launched the H.O.P.E. Project (Handling Overwhelming Pressures Effectively), with its primary mission of building critical support networks, providing tangible opportunities, and implementing strategic progressive goals for underserved youth and their families.

Some local officials are very open about the fact that there is a gang presence in their community. Some are less likely to talk about it. But gang investigators around the state say if you have drugs in your community, you have gangs.

Drugs have been around since the foundation of the U.S. as have drug problems.

After the Civil War, soldiers from the armies of both the North and the South often had a hard time finding work. Forged in the heat of epic military battles and skilled in the use of firearms, some veterans, like Jesse James, used their military skills to become outlaws and bandits. Many civil war vets suffered from the "soldiers disease" (morphine addiction) and roamed the streets in gangs begging and stealing to survive. After the assassination of President Lincoln these men rioted in Washington D.C., requiring the military to put down the riots and secure the peace.

The problem of gangs in the military has been studied in recent years by such individuals such as Officer Scott Barfield of Renton PD in Washington State, Retired Corrections Sgt. Jeff Stoleson in the Mid-West, and Retired L.A. County Sheriff's Department Sgt. Richard Valdemar. These individuals, and a few others, exposed this major problem in the nation's armed forces even though the military brass first denied it.

Hunter "Gator" Glass, a retired police detective and gang expert in Fayetteville, N.C., home to Fort Bragg and the 82nd Airborne, knows of members of many gang members who served in the military. Glass points out, "The military is merely a reflection of the society it serves. As gangs grow in the U.S., they will grow somewhat comparatively in the military."

College Professor, Dr. Carter F. Smith studied gangs in the military for years after first discovering the problem as a criminal investigator in the Army. While one independent study shows less than one-percent of service members are in gangs, Smith says that is still far too many. "If there's a million and a half people in the military, less than one-percent is how many? Fifteen-thousand. Are you okay with 15,000 people trained to kill, maim?" he asks.

Smith believes most gang members join the military to get away from the gang, then find it difficult to break away. He fears what might happen when military training, weapons and equipment are combined with a gang creed. Drug running, intimidation, violence, Smith says, all are possibilities.

Gang members have been known in recent years to come from the military and to infiltrate police departments, using tactics and information they learn there to both outsmart and confront law enforcement and rival gangs.

In addition to military members who kept their gang affiliations at numerous bases across the southeast United States, there is the problem of military dependents. Many of these kids go to school in medium to small sized towns just off base that often have an "us vs. them" mentality. Communities like military members and their children who spend money in local businesses but also sometimes have a grudge against them as outsiders.

This rings true even more so with military dependents. Many of them moved into the area and did not grow up with the local kids, so there is less bonding. They are also often viewed as outsiders. To fit in they may join a local gang or form a gang they brought with them from another area or create one for protection.

Christina "Queenie" Walters was a 14 year old military dependent who lived off base at Fort Bragg in North Carolina. She became the leader of a local Crips gang in Fayetteville, NC. She was convicted in the August 17, 1988, murders of 18-year-old Tracy Lambert and 21-year-old Susan Moore. Walters was also tried for the attempted murder of Debra Cheeseborough. She later admitted to shooting several .32-caliber bullets into Cheeseborough and thinking she had successfully killed her. The murders were done as a gang-initiation and the victims were chosen at random. Walters and her accomplices, Eric Queen and Francisco "Paco" Tirado, were later convicted and given the death penalty for their crimes. Walters had her death sentence commuted and is now doing a life sentence in a North Carolina woman's prison.

Some experts have referred to the growing popularity of motorcycle clubs as the "Sons of Anarchy" syndrome. Many Outlaw Motorcycle Gangs (OMG) looked at

99% of these individuals as being just "Weekend Warriors". They state they do not live and breathe the Biker lifestyle but mimic national more well-known clubs. This includes the growing number of "law enforcement or retired police" clubs.

Outlaw Motorcycle Gangs are present in the South and expanding. They like to call themselves Motorcycle Clubs (MC), but many of their members engage in criminal activity and proudly proclaim themselves to be 1%ers.

Alabama is a Bandido MC state. Pisoleros MC are a support club of the Bandits. Their color are yellow and red but reverse, yellow on a red background, while Bandidos have red on a yellow background. Hells Angels do not have a current presence in Alabama but that may soon change as Devils Disciples (largest club in Alabama) is considered a support club for the HAs. Of course, the Hells Angels continue to enjoy a share of the control the Carolinas and Virginia and they have an active support club in Arkansas known as the 501 Crew which is based on the central Arkansas area code "501".

The southeastern United States is still predominately controlled by the Outlaws with a strong presence in Florida, Georgia, Alabama, Tennessee, Arkansas, Kentucky, Virginia and the Carolina's. With that being said the Mongols have been rapidly expanding while growing their existing chapters in Florida and Virginia and adding charters in Arkansas, Tennessee and North Carolina. The Outlaws and Mongols have maintained a friendly relationship and there are no indications on the horizon of that changing. The Pagans have been more aggressive in recruiting in Florida over the past few years and although they maintain a presence in Kentucky and West Virginia they are in no ways dominant in the southeast.

The Vagos have established in Georgia and the Sons of Silence have chapters in Florida, Mississippi, Kentucky, Arkansas and Louisiana.

Two separate factions of the Warlocks operate within the southeast and they remain at odds although there has not been a major incident between the two since the 2012 shooting in Winter Springs, Florida where four members of the "Northern" Warlocks shot and killed three members of the "Southern" Warlocks. The Northern Warlocks who hail from Philadelphia formed in 1967 and wear a symbol referred to as "Harpie" for their center patch. The Southern Warlocks formed in 1967 in Florida and have a center patch that is a Phoenix/War Bird. Both Warlocks clubs have a presence in Florida while the "Southern" Warlocks also operate in Georgia, South Carolina, Virginia and West Virginia.

The most interesting development in the past few years is the expansion of International Outlaw Motorcycle Gangs into the US with more than one planting a flag in the southeast. The Rebels which are the largest 1% OMG in Australia were the first to establish and now another well-known Australian OMG called the Comancheros has arrived. The expansion of these groups into the US will no doubt create issues with the US based OMG'S.

There are even African-American OMGs like the Outcast and Wheels of Soul (WOS). The WOS in the past few years made a footprint in the central region, but for the most part everyone seems to get along at Biker rallies. That could change if new groups keep moving in on established ones.

 **Aryan Circle Motorcycle Club (MC)**

The Galloping Goose MC is active in Louisiana as well as the Sons of Silence Motorcycle Club (SOSMC). They also have an Aryan Circle Motorcycle Club (MC) active within the state. Like the AC prison gang they often use a 1-3 handsign for the 1st letter (A) and third letter (C) of the alphabet.

Law Enforcement Actions and Resources

Birmingham PD and others in the state were often in denial and ignored the gangs after they calmed-down after the 1980s and early 90s gang epidemic.

Law enforcement, in conjunction with local politicians, have now devised new local and state laws to deal with the growing and resurging gang epidemic.

Florida State Statue 874 covers defines criminal gangs, gang members, and gang associates. It then provides for enhanced penalties for crimes committed in furtherance of the interests of a gang; new statutes for recruiting gang members; and a new crime allowing the charging of a Gang Kingpin for directing the activities of a gang. There is also a newly redrafted provision that allows cities to enter injunctions against gang activity at a specific location. Much like the violation of a domestic violence injunction, the violation of a gang injunction can also result in arrest for violating the terms of the injunction.

Law enforcement has found that having Gang Units can be very effective in their battle against street crimes and violence. The Nashville Specialized Investigations Division's Gang Unit combats gang related crime through active suppression, investigation, and intelligence gathering. Information is collected by various means to determine if these individuals or groups might be a threat to Nashville. The Gang Unit investigates crimes that are reported as gang related (such as assault, vandalism, narcotic related, etc.). The Gang Unit also has the responsibility for distributing analyzed data on gang matters and focusing on criminal violations committed by criminal gangs. The Gang Unit also shares this information and works with other agencies including the FBI, DEA, ATF, ICE, and other law enforcement agencies.

Investigative entities and intelligence units have long been vital in mitigating gang activity. Agencies at every level of law enforcement continue to join forces to combat gang violence, and remain committed to combating gangs, as gang activity continues to threaten communities nationwide.

Founded in 1998, the Tennessee Gang Investigators Association (TNGIA) includes Local, State, and Federal Law Enforcement, Corrections, and Court System Professionals whose interest or primary investigative responsibilities include the identification and prosecution of crimes related to gang activity.

The Alabama Gang Investigators Association (AGIA) was founded in 2010 to address the growing gang problem in Alabama. AGIA provides information, training and other resources to those in law enforcement, corrections, juvenile justice, District Attorneys, education and more importantly, to the citizens of Alabama. The AGIA promotes a free exchange of information, education and intelligence to reduce the scourge that is gangs.

The Georgia Gang Investigators Association (GGIA), was founded in 1998, as the organization to combat the uprising of gang violence in Georgia. The purpose of the GGIA is to promote a free exchange of intelligence and information among investigators, with the goal of effectively impacting on the level of gang related violence perpetrated by criminal groups, whose actions affect and constitute a threat to public order.

The North Carolina Gang Investigators Association is made up of law enforcement and criminal justice professionals who are dedicated to the prevention of gangs and suppression of gang-related activity within the state of North Carolina. Through enhanced inter-agency intelligence exchange, legislative activism, citizen awareness, innovative anti-gang operational tactics, and by providing professional education and training, NCGIA plays a significant role in creating a safer environment for residents and visitors

The South Carolina Gang Investigators Association is a professional organization composed of criminal justice professionals from throughout the state. They are dedicated to the prevention, intervention, and suppression of criminal threat groups, extremists or terrorist groups, and outlaw gang activity throughout South Carolina..

The Florida Gang Investigator's Association (FGIA) was formed in 1993, by criminal justice professionals, FGIA provides a professional organization for all those within the criminal justice system who share a common goal of intervening, preventing and enforcing suppression against criminal gang activity. This mission will be carried out through enhanced interagency intelligence exchange, legislative activism, citizen awareness, innovative anti-gang awareness operational tactics and by providing professional education and training.

Recent criminal cases seem to indicate Mississippi has a significant gang presence and authorities are pushing for more resources and focus to combat them. The Legislature is going to have to be able to support cities whose budgets are already strained, and with law enforcement officers already having a difficult time to bring more assets to bear on the gang problems that exist there," officials say.

Jimmy Anthony, Mississippi Assoc. of Gang Inv. Vice President, agreed. "The time for deniability is past. We've got to face the problem at hand and implement the laws that need to be put there to deal with the situations as they are arising."

As gangs grow in number, power, and drug sales they get busted by regional, state, and federal gang task forces. As they get introduced into state and federal prison systems they usually find themselves alone or with just a few homeboys who they can trust. They are often victimized by the larger national gangs and forced to join an alliance or join a prison gang. When they get out they have been indoctrinated, learn the advantages of having back-up on a state and national scale.

Some local officials are very open about the fact that there is a gang presence in their community. Some are less likely to talk about it. But gang investigators around the state say if you have drugs in your community, you have gangs.

Drugs have been around since the foundation of the U.S. as have drug problems.

After the Civil War, soldiers from the armies of both the North and the South often had a hard time finding work. Forged in the heat of epic military battles and skilled in the use of firearms, some veterans, like Jesse James, used their military skills to become outlaws and bandits. Many civil war vets suffered from the "soldiers disease" (morphine addiction) and roamed the streets in gangs begging and stealing to survive. After the assassination of President Lincoln these men rioted in Washington D.C., requiring the military to put down the riots and secure the peace.

The problem of gangs in the military has been studied in recent years by Officer Scott Barfield of Renton PD in Washington State, Retired Corrections Sgt. Jeff Stoleson in the Mid-West, and Retired L.A. County Sheriff's Department Sgt. Richard Valdemar. These individuals, and a few others, exposed this major problem in the nation's armed forces even though the military brass first denied it.

Hunter "Gator" Glass, a retired police detective and gang expert in Fayetteville, N.C., home to Fort Bragg and the 82nd Airborne, knows of members of many gang members who served in the military. Glass points out, "The military is merely a reflection of the society it serves. As gangs grow in the U.S., they will grow somewhat comparatively in the military."

College Professor, Dr. Carter F. Smith studied gangs in the military for years after first discovering the problem as a criminal investigator in the Army. While one independent study shows less than one-percent of service members are in gangs, Smith says that is still far too many. "If there's a million and a half people in the military, less than one-percent is how many? Fifteen-thousand. Are you okay with 15,000 people trained to kill, maim?" he asks.

Smith believes most gang members join the military to get away from the gang, then find it difficult to break away. He fears what might happen when military training, weapons and equipment are combined with a gang creed. Drug running, intimidation, violence, Smith says, all are possibilities.

Gang members have been known in recent years to come from the military and to infiltrate police departments, using tactics and information they learn there to both outsmart and confront law enforcement and rival gangs.

In addition to military members who kept their gang affiliations at numerous bases across the southeast United States, there is the problem of military dependents. Many of these kids go to school in medium to small sized towns just off base that often have an "us vs. them" mentality. Communities like military members and their children who spend money in local businesses but also sometimes have a grudge against them as outsiders. This rings true even more so with military dependents. Many of them moved into the area and did not grow up with the local kids, so there is less bonding. They are also often viewed as outsiders. To fit in they may join a local gang or form a gang they brought with them from another area or create one for protection.

Gangs are domestic terrorists both out on streets and in prisons, said Capt. Vincent Goggins, Richland County, S.C. deputy who heads the Midlands Gang Task Force.

Members today decide deliberately to join a gang, unlike in the past when it was something new to try, Goggins says.

They are moving away from dealing drugs and weapons in favor of white-collar crime, such as counterfeit money, credit card fraud, tax fraud and human trafficking, Goggins said.

As you can see by now, there are a wide variety of gangs in the Southern States of the U.S., and they are far more active than most people are aware of.

Hopefully this book has helped better explain past tensions and modern dynamics in southern society.

Again, the South has always been a land of rebels. Slavery made a lasting scar upon it. War, poverty, and gang violence have afflicted many people too long.

As we stated in the beginning, street gangs are often formed as the result of marginalization, limiting access to social and economic conditions.

But, we have faith that the South "will rise up again". By that we mean, rise up against these groups that prey on their communities.

The vast majority of people in the South are good people. The vast majority of cops are good cops.

Only by working together against gangs and disruptive groups will we be able to turn the tide against crime, lessen their impact, and make communities safe.

Sources:

Alabama Gangs, Alabama Gang Investigator's Association, 2015

More Augusta gangs affiliating with national groups, Augusta Chronicle, 7/21/12

Gang wars: Officials say resources needed to fight gangs, Carion Ledger, 7/14/16

Mid-West Outlaw Motorcycle Gang Inv. Asoc, Steve Cook, 2015

Police unit steers kids away from gangs, Gainesville Sun, 10/29/16

Hunter Glass Interview, 2016

National Gang Report, National Gang Intelligence Center, 2015

Gangs, RISS, 2016

SC gangs evolving, switching to white collar crime, The State, 8/8/16

Local group lures young people away from gangs, Times Free Press 11/28/15

Criminal Gangs in the Military, Richard Valdemar, 2007

Gangsters, Bikers, and Terrorists in the Military, Carter F. Smith, (TBD)

Acknowledgments

Tami Jo Aiken, Tim Ayers, Kimberly Bell, Justin Brown, Steve Cook, Ernest Cuthbertson, Jose Diaz, Marcos Flores, Robert Fountain, James "Hoot" Gibson, Cory Godwin, Juan Gonzalez, Louis Guiden, Chuck Hastings, Johnny Hawkins, Carter Hickman, Tom Howard, Michelle Jordan, James "Rusty" Keeble, Korey Kooper, TJ Leyden, Christopher Long, Robert Mateo, Mark Pitcavage, Jeffrey P. Rush, Marco Silva, Shawn Williams, the National Gang Intelligence Center, and especially to Dr. Carter F. Smith, Adam Schniper, and F. Hunter Glass.

Definitions

At-Risk Youth – A young person one who is less likely to transition into adulthood successfully. Success is frequently defined as the ability to avoid crime, achieve academic success, and become financially independent. Could bat at risk to join gangs.

Wanna-B/Gonna-B- A youth often viewed as a poser, follower, not real, who copies or imitates a gang member. The reality is, if intervention is not done, the youth is likely to engage in criminal behaviors to get respect and viewed a "Real G".

Street Gangs/G-Can mean any combination, confederation, alliance, network, conspiracy, understanding, or other similar arrangement in law or in fact, of three or more persons that, through its membership or through the agency of any member, engages in a course or pattern of criminal activity. A "G" is a gangster.

Prison Gangs-Is an inmate organization that operates within a prison system, that has a corporate entity, exists into perpetuity, and whose membership is restrictive, mutually exclusive, and often requires a lifetime commitment.

Security Threat Group-Basically any gang or group inside jails and prison that may present a risk to safety and security.

Disruptive Groups-This term is sometimes used to describe groups that may not be a prison gang but still present a disruptive threat to safety and security.

Organized Crime-Is illegal behavior that is planned and carried out by groups of people in a very systematic and sophisticated fashion. An example of organized crime is the activities of money laundering done by the Mafia/La Cosa Nostra.

www.ingramcontent.com/pod-product-compliance
Lightning Source LLC
Chambersburg PA
CBHW070151290526
45789CB00002B/726